All Who Belong May Enter

Nicholas Ward

Winner of the Autumn House Nonfiction Prize

AUTUMN
HOUSE PRESS

All
Who
Belong
May
Enter

ISBN: 978-1-938769-96-2
LCCN: 2021939766

autumnhouse.org

"Autumn House Press" and "Autumn House" are registered trademarks
owned by Autumn House Press, a nonprofit corporation whose mission is
the publication and promotion of poetry and other fine literature.

 Autumn House Press receives state arts funding
support through a grant from the Pennsylvania
Council on the Arts, a state agency funded by the
Commonwealth of Pennsylvania, and the National
Endowment for the Arts, a federal agency.

Typeset in Addington CF
Book and cover design by Peter Barnfather
Cover photography by Taylor Wilcox / taywilphoto.com

All Autumn House books are printed on acid-free paper
and meet the international standards of permanent books
intended for purchase by libraries.

Printed in the USA

To my parents, whom I deeply love even though I overwhelm them.

To Patti, forever and ever and ever.

Contents

I CAN ALWAYS BE FOUND

Boys Always Play at Killing Each Other

Watch Him Go

When I was a boy, I fell in love with an athlete. I wasn't the only one. In 1989, this man—barely past being a teenager himself—electrified the national football scene as a running back for the Oklahoma State Cowboys. A year later, he was selected third overall in the NFL draft by the Detroit Lions, my family's football team.

My dad used to tell me that the Lions might never be good again but that Barry Sanders made them special. I've still never seen anyone run like him. He'd smash his body through a mass of behemoths, a gladiator in Honolulu blue, smaller than everyone. He'd ping from one corner of the field to the next, legs churning, body twisting and turning while his opponents tried to smother him, to pound him to the turf. He was relentless. He might be stopped at the line on fifteen straight occasions. But that sixteenth time? He'd bust an eighty-yard run for a score, untouched, his legs scissoring across the green Astroturf. Or he might appear to go down, but he'd ever so delicately place his fingers on the grass, spring back up, and power into the end zone. One early fall afternoon, playing against the Bears at Soldier Field, he barreled into a cloud of tacklers, subsumed into their expanse. Players on the periphery slowed to a jog, assuming the play over, but Barry somehow emerged from the pile like a rocket, sprinting to another touchdown. I can't find the run anywhere on YouTube. It's like I dreamed it.

After every single score, he'd calmly hand the football to the official. "You see that?" my dad would say, watching the Lions with me on Sundays after church. "He doesn't showboat or spike it. He respects the game."

In 1991, the Lions won their six final games and then crushed the Dallas Cowboys on their way to the conference title game. At ten years old, I'd never seen my father more excited. It was the Lions' first championship game since 1957, a decade before the Super Bowl began, when my dad was just an eight-year-old in the suburbs of Detroit. For the 1991 contest against the Washington Football Team—back then they were still called the offensive slur they eventually changed—my dad set the VCR to record and then controlled the remote, a small rectangle affixed via a thick cord to the device, that allowed him to pause and start recording. He wanted only to capture the game. No commercials. No timeouts. Just football.

Detroit lost 41-10 to Washington that day. We didn't know that loss would be the high point of the franchise. Being hopeless fans of the Lions was an identity we wore whether we asked for it or not.

On most fall weekday afternoons in my childhood, I spent the time between the afternoon school bell and dinner throwing the pigskin around with the neighborhood boys on my suburban block. None of us were very good, though I didn't know that back then. I fancied myself the fastest and quickest of the bunch, the four to eight of us who regularly played, and I took Barry Sanders as my inspiration. If he was small and successful, then I could be too. From Barry, it was a natural progression to other players: the majesty of Jerry Rice, the toughness of Bruce Smith, the creativity of Junior Seau. I consumed it all. I'd spend Sundays in front of the television. Monday nights, I begged my parents to let me stay up late; my dad and I watched playoffs perched in the family room. And in the off-seasons, I devoured the details of the previous year, watching replays, studying stats. One season, I taped every single highlight from ESPN's *NFL Primetime*; that was back when the telecast aired once a week, and each segment received a three- to four-minute highlight, telling the story of each contest. I even taped the *SportsCenter*s that weren't featured on Sundays, so there would be a clear progression and inclusion of the Sunday night game, Monday Night Football, Thanksgiving Day, and those random Saturday games.

I started playing real football in the fall of 1994, at the age of thirteen, donning pads and a helmet for the first time for the Farmington Rockets, a local organization affiliated with a league scattered throughout the Detroit suburbs. I was bad. I knew I was small, of course. But I was slow, too, which surprised me, and anxious under pressure. On the first snap of my very first game, the opposing team threw a pass to the tight end. From my safety position towards the back of the defense, it was my job to break up the pass, to bat it down. Instead, I grabbed the tight end by the back of his shoulder pads and yanked him down, earning a fifteen-yard penalty and scorn from my irate coach.

"At least you didn't let him catch it," my dad shrugged after the game.

Twenty years later, when I started working on this essay, I asked my mom why, knowing my stature, they let me play.

Nicholas Ward

"You really wanted to," she answered.
"If I was a child now, with all the knowledge about concussions and CTE, would you let me?" I asked.
"Probably not."
The only time I really felt like I belonged to the Rockets was the night before the last game of the season, when the girls on the cheerleading squad toilet papered my house, an organizational ritual. With the boys, it was more complicated. On the field one game, I missed a tackle that led to a touchdown, and no one spoke to me the rest of the day. When I didn't practice the day that I got braces, Mike Jones—the starting middle linebacker—made fun of me. "I practiced the day I got braces," he said. "Of course, I'm not a sissy."

For five years, from middle school until I went to college, my father and I attended at least one Lions' game a season. When they went on sale in late July, we'd drive over to the stadium and buy tickets. We didn't need to make the trek; my dad could've ordered them over the phone. But he didn't like paying the exorbitant markup fees, and his job as a teacher gave him the time to make the journey. I think he loved looking at the map of the stadium and choosing our seats, putting his finger right on the square and saying, "We want these." My father didn't grow up poor, but his family was working-class enough that the purchase of one-to-four games' worth of football tickets would have constituted a luxury. I think he liked calling out that he'd made it, that he could offer me more.

On game days, we'd park in downtown Pontiac, another Rust Belt community a half hour away from ours. We'd leave the car at a place called the Phoenix Center and board a bus with other fans. This was when the team played at the old Pontiac Silverdome. We always sat in the same seats: the second row in the corners of the upper deck where there was no first row and we could get in and out without disturbing anyone—just a quick

6

duck under the support bars. They really were great seats. We got a perfect view of the action, but more than anything, I remember being in the crowd, the way we'd rise to our feet when a play broke open, a tidal wave of whooping and hollering.

Barry Sanders retired in 1999, after a decade of service to the Lions. He was at the very apex of his career, one year away from breaking Walter Payton's all-time rushing record. He didn't hold a press conference; instead, he faxed a letter to his hometown newspaper, the *Wichita Eagle*, as quiet and unassuming a gesture as all those times he handed the ball to the official when he scored a touchdown. Mitch Albom, the longtime *Detroit Free Press* reporter, wrote that "Sanders' departure has deep ramifications for this city, its football team, even its image." I find this ironic, given that Barry only set foot in downtown Detroit in the form of a fourteen-story mural on the side of the Cadillac Tower; he played all of his home games in a suburb outside the city.

Fans wanted more. How could he turn his back on us? On the game? His team? We, the fans, wanted to decide when Barry finished playing. Because he electrified us, and we were devoted to watching him, we thought we had a say in the matter. We blamed the franchise for destroying Barry Sanders's career. The Lions never surrounded him with a team good enough to win more than one playoff game or a coach skilled enough to take advantage of the talent they did have. But maybe we killed his career. Maybe we expected too much from him. Maybe it's our fault and we did not know it and we did not want to know it.

After Barry retired, the Lions started to really suck. His exodus, combined with a host of other factors, spun them down a rabbit hole of ten straight losing seasons and the worst winning percentage in football. Being a Lions fan is an exercise in constant heartbreak. When Calvin Johnson, their most recent star player, walked away a half-decade ago, that seemed like as good a time as any to stop investing time into the team.

Nicholas Ward

I have a perilous relationship with football, whether it's the college game, with universities making millions off unpaid labor, or the NFL and its blind eye towards concussions and mental health, Orwellian drug policy, pervasive rape and domestic violence culture, absurd on-the-field "scandals," blowhard media coverage, excessive game length, and obvious blackballing of its most famous ex-player. Football was never pure. In order to watch this sport, I must extinguish parts of myself that care about the damage it inflicts upon the bodies and minds of the men who play it, the women who live alongside them, and the fans who devote hours and money in larger quantities every year.

There was so much I didn't understand about the game at the time I fell in love with it. I didn't understand why mostly Black men brought us sodas and hot dogs, took tickets at the turnstiles, but mostly white people sat in the stands with us. I didn't understand why the Detroit Lions played their home games in Pontiac, thirty miles north of the city from whom they took their name and their mythos, why they'd moved out to the suburbs in the mid-1970s with the last of the white businesses. Later, I would come to recognize that watching football is as much about rooting for the destruction of men as it is celebrating their success. And I would try to grapple with the anti-Blackness baked into that destruction and that celebration.

I can't distance myself as much as I wish I could. I, too, pleaded at the top of my lungs with the players on the field, imploring them to run faster, jump higher, hit harder. When the stadium was buzzing and Barry Sanders was flying down the field, I felt like I belonged to something.

8

Miles Apart

My aunt and uncle once owned a Christmas tree farm in my father's hometown of Milford, Michigan. Technically belonging to my aunt's side of the family, and thus not in my lineage, the Broadview Christmas Tree Farm is 118 acres of Scotch pines, spruces, and Douglas firs, among other varieties of trees. Every year, on the day after Thanksgiving, my parents and I would pile into our blue minivan and drive the forty-five minutes from my hometown in search of the perfect tree. The scenery during this journey was magnificent to my young eyes. When we finally pulled onto Hickory Ridge Road, I was in heaven: houses furlongs apart, overgrown bramble, empty and dilapidated barns, and other cars so infrequent, suggesting total solitude. Our minivan would glide over the hills, rolling up and down, while I stared out the side window at the sparse landscape. We'd approach the last, impossible hill, towards the arch of forest dense with plush trees that looked like they'd survived centuries. We'd turn off through the woods, lumbering down a gravel drive that opened onto a clearing where my cousin, Aaron, and some of his buddies would direct traffic, parking the cars in fine rows. Aaron's dad, my uncle Jim, once the star running back at Milford High, took out groups on flatbed trailers, bouncing the group through the farm to find their own perfect Christmas tree. My aunt Marty commandeered operations in the barn, fixing batches of fried chicken. Beth, Aaron's older sister, made sure enough silverware was stocked and poured hot cider for the local families.

At the end of the day, the whole family on both sides would retire to Marty and Jim's house across the street—not exactly across—there was no neat jaunt out there like there was in our suburb. We had to go back up the gravel hill, over Hickory Ridge Road, turn down Broadview Lane, and drive a half-mile through the woods, where the trees parted to reveal the gorgeous house my uncle built, the A-frame design, an angled roof that shot skyward like a church steeple. Around back, a long deck hung over a wide ravine. It was quiet and isolated.

I was never able to articulate it in such a way, but I wondered back then if there was a touch of defiance in living so far out in the country, away from the hubbub and the consumerism. It may have taken longer to retrieve a quart of milk, but they didn't need all that other crap, just a simple existence in the middle of nowhere.

My parents and I lived in Farmington, one ring of the Detroit suburbs that looked like all the others, in a one-story ranch house with a courteously mowed yard and brick siding. It was nothing compared to the log palace my uncle and older cousins occupied in the woods. Driving west from our Chatham Hills subdivision, we'd fly past a mini-mall, bank, gas station, car dealership, another mini-mall, bowling alley, another mini-mall, the venerable bar and grill Dunleavy's, another mini-mall, a cemetery, and a funeral home, before arriving at the cute downtown with its two-dollar movie theatre, local ice cream shop, and long-standing delis and Italian restaurants. All the assorted landmarks of suburban sprawl.

In 1993, on my mother's birthday, Uncle Jim called to announce that he'd asked Marty, his wife of twenty-three years, for a divorce. That same year, we discovered that I had severe allergies to the trees that grew on Broadview farm. My parents switched to a fake Christmas tree, unfurled from a box that they keep in the basement. For years, my dad and I unfolded the tree together, sitting on the floor watching college football, peeling the prickly branches apart.

My cousin Aaron later built his own house in the woods, on the Broadview property. His solitude seems sinister to me now. It's land that's belonged in his family for a hundred years, and Aaron proudly displays a wooden placard announcing the deed of the sale. I'm not certain he knows who owned the land before that. Aaron is a cop by profession and a hunter by hobby; he and his wife, Katherine, watch Fox News, regurgitating the rhetoric of the conservative teleprompter. Their only neighbors are the cousins who live on the other side of the ridge, a four-wheeler's trip away.

Before the 2016 election, my parents were visiting Aaron and Katherine and their kids for dinner. At some point in the evening, I'm told, my father suggested that, as white people, we didn't understand what it was like to be Black in America. Aaron flew into a rage, shouting at my father, insisting that he didn't know what he was talking about. When my mom jumped in to argue that Black people get pulled over by the cops just for being Black, Katherine turned on her, accusing her of falling for the liberal conspiracy. This verbal abuse shook my parents, how quickly their nephew and his wife turned to anger, how violently they exposed their racism.

Nicholas Ward

I haven't had a relationship with my cousin in a long time. Aaron once visited Chicago and tried to get me to have drinks with him in the Loop, where only tourists and finance workers hang out, but I declined when I easily could have arranged to meet him. I think I've seen him twice in the past ten years, on back-to-back Christmas Eves. The men talked about guns, on which I can contribute nothing, or we all chimed in on the Red Wings, of whom I know a little more. I admire that Aaron will kill a deer during hunting season that will help feed his family for six months. Maybe he'd be jealous that I can shop at a half dozen different grocery stores in a few miles radius and get everything I need easily to make chana masala or Hungarian paprikash. If we had a relationship, maybe we'd see a bit more in each other that we didn't already know. Maybe we'd be at each other's throats from each side of our political, social, and cultural divide. It's possible we'd just as easily express politeness publicly and grievances privately. We don't talk on the phone or text, we aren't friends on Facebook, and if my parents quizzed me about Aaron's children, I would fail the test. I know I should feel guilty that I've let the relationship slip this far. But I don't.

Firepower

The first boy I knew who died by suicide was named John. He was the older brother of a girl in my grade, a high school sophomore to us seventh graders. I hardly knew John but I recall him as cocky and arrogant, a popular kid.

It happened on the first Sunday of football season, Labor Day weekend. The Lions beat the Atlanta Falcons in overtime that afternoon. The game played on the radio as my parents and I visited their friends, who lived on a docked houseboat on the lake, a small floating pontoon that rocked slightly in the Lake Huron water. Fake grass, like you'd see at a mini-golf course, covered the back patio. My childhood best friend, Ryan, and I spent the afternoon outside, me wanting to play football and him determined to catch frogs. We were damn near inseparable around that time, though so dissimilar, it's a wonder we remained friends for so long.

My mom called me from outside to watch the local evening news. A solemn-looking man with a microphone stood outside a two-story house in a subdivision near ours and told the viewing audience of the tragedy contained therein, a fatal shooting, an accident.

We'd known John's family for years, everyone did in our corner of the universe—our little patch of gravel, where we'd grown up together on the ball fields and blacktops, riding our bikes through town or walking the streets on hot summer afternoons.

On John's quiet suburban street, only one person knew what really happened. The story we were told as news and gossip was that John, a skilled hunter, was handling a firearm that exploded in his face. His friend, Mike, sat next to him. John had been showing him something with the gun, had accidentally pointed it towards his head, and somehow pulled the trigger. No one else was home, not his mother or three younger sisters. The parents had long divorced, the gun case the only remnant of the father. John obviously had a key, taking the guns out for hunting weekends. I'd never set foot inside the house, so I could only imagine where he did it, where the guns were kept, out in the garage maybe or the den.

It made no sense, we all wondered aloud. Why would a kid raised with respect for weapons, for the power they unleashed, commit such a reckless act? What would he need to show Mike in that exact moment? Maybe there was a struggle and the gun went off. Maybe he was in love with his own power. Maybe he wanted to die. We never found out. Mike disappeared for a few years, and when he returned, there were whispers but no confrontations. The town could be cruel but not that cruel.

After John, there was Dusty. After Dusty, there was Raif. And those were the only ones I knew. How many towns were just like mine? What makes a boy decide it's just not worth it anymore?

Now that I'm older, I wonder if it could have been me. I felt so lonely, growing up in that suburban enclave. Sure, there are fond memories of crushes and baseball games. But as I got older, I realized I didn't want the world I'd grown up in. I didn't yet have the language or the history to understand how that world was constructed, built by and for people who looked like me but strangling us inside it all the same. I allowed sadness to linger in my chest, lodge itself in my gullet.

It would have been so easy. There were always weapons about. Sometimes it felt like every step I took was on a tightrope wire. That's how the loneliness engulfed me. I don't know if it consumed those other boys, though I know now that the loneliness followed me forever: into college and adulthood, surrounded by great friends or making dinner by myself, in and out of love more times than is generally thought acceptable, in the winter and the spring and the morning and the night. It's the loneliness that will always be the one constant.

The First Game

We parked on Michigan Avenue, like we always would, walking hand-in-hand through Corktown, the oldest neighborhood in Detroit. We bought peanuts in brown paper bags from vendors on the street. They were more expensive inside the ballpark, but I didn't know that then. "I think these ones taste better," my dad always said.

It was May 1, 1988. I was in kindergarten. The Tigers won ninety-eight games the season before, earning an AL East crown, just four years removed from their latest World Series victory.

Our seats were down the left field foul line, where my dad had season tickets that he shared with a group of men and their sons. The vendors shouted back and forth across the stadium, from left field to right, a call-and-response hawking "Ice Cold

Cokes!" for no good reason other than it was almost summer and going to heat up soon and there are eighty-two home games a year. Time must be passed somehow.

Tiger Stadium was, even then, a crumbling masterpiece, all rusted steel and busted concrete, obstructed views behind the blue beams that anchored the outfield stands, seats that rose straight up, so you felt close to the action, no matter where you sat.

My dad told me years later that I screamed nearly the whole game, yelling myself hoarse behind an older woman who didn't seem to mind one bit. Matt Nokes, the Tigers' promising young catcher, hit two home runs against the Mariners in a come-from-behind victory, but I wasn't awake for either of them. I cheered so unrelentingly in the first few innings that I knocked myself to sleep. My dad carried me to the car after the game, like he would so many nights of my childhood, when we were out late visiting relatives or returning from the haunted Halloween pumpkin patch or church services on Christmas Eve. We'd pull into the driveway of our one-story rambler, the sound of the garage door jarring me awake in the back seat. "Okay, pal," my dad would say in his homegrown Michigan accent, "we're home."

I don't remember the exact day and opponent and box score of that first game. But I know Matt Nokes hit two home runs, and my dad insisted the game was in early May. A quick Baseball-Reference search finds that Nokes only once hit two homers as a Tiger that early in the season: May 1, 1988, a 3-2 victory against the Seattle Mariners. I like being able to pinpoint this. If everything else exists only in memory—where we parked, the peanuts, the stadium's crumbling facade—the game is fixed, recorded, and set down for all time, exactly .012 percent of all games played at Tiger Stadium. A blip. Another day at the ballpark. If the box score didn't exist, it would be like it never happened. We need validation. *See*, we get to say, *we were there. We remember.*

Nicholas Ward

I have begun to recognize that continuing to love baseball means understanding the sport's tangled history of racism and classism. It means knowing that Major League Baseball was built on segregation and that integration didn't change the racism in its roots. It means holding some affection for the 1919 White Sox, the greatest team of their era, who threw the World Series after getting screwed out of the money owed to them. It means arguing with my father that the highest-paid players deserve their salaries —and probably more—because of how much money they make for the men who sign their checks. It means analyzing baseball as a tool of US imperialism and nationalism and still loving the crack of the bat in Game 7 of the World Series. Yes, the season is too long. I'll still watch the final outs anyway.

That first game: before I collected stacks of baseball cards; before I grew to admire and then abhor other teams; before I realized I loved a game of failure that was destined to break my heart; before I cataloged seasons and players and stats in my brain, filing them away for later, when I will meet others like me, obsessives who romanticize the game beyond all reason, sons and daughters, nieces and nephews, who tell stories of their own games, with fathers and mothers and uncles and aunts and friends, stories we collect so that we can share them, like so many other myths of American life.

I'd recall the specifics of other baseball games better: missing both of Cleveland's designated hitter Jim Thome's monster home runs because I went searching for all-star ballots; Cecil Fielder's big blasts the season he hit fifty-one, and my aunt Judy visiting from Phoenix, jumping up and down like a little kid because "I just want to see him hit one"; when my buddy Ryan's stepfather made us leave early, but then we got boxed in on all sides in the parking lot and listened to Mikey Tettleton's walk-off, extra-inning shot on the radio while sitting directly outside the stadium. But there's something about the way that first game sits in my

18

memory: a little hazy around the edges, hard to articulate, powerful precisely because I can't fully recall it.

These days, the land at the corner of Michigan and Trumbull is The Corner Ballpark presented by Adient, the official field of the Detroit Police Athletic League. Tiger Stadium held so much promise once. Even after it was demolished and sold for scraps, the land could have been a public park for kids to roam freely or affordable housing in an increasingly unaffordable city. But no, like everything else in our liberal cities, cops receive their accoutrements, no questions asked, while everybody else competes for what's left. Some of the old steel gates still fortress the area, but it's difficult to recall this land as hallowed ground for Midwestern sports fans. It looks so small now, that patch of grass, as if I could still get a group of boys together and shag fly balls in the fading afternoon sun.

There Is No Violence Here

Each afternoon that fall, I suited up for my daily submission to brutality, otherwise known as freshman football. I was fifteen years old. I'd never smoked a cigarette or gotten drunk or had sex. I possessed neither speed nor strength, neither catching nor tackling ability. Practice was my chance to shine.

One Thursday, in the middle of a light-contact scrimmage, a routine running play broke open, and Brian B. bore down on me. Brian was a hulking behemoth of a kid, a head taller and seventy-five pounds heavier than me. Brian, who once punched a hole through a cinder block column in a fit of anger, mauled opposing players as a blocker and a runner. Once you got into his sights, it was probably best to get out of the way.

I tried to tackle him low.

He cleaned my clock so completely that I fell flat on my back, staring through the bars of my helmet at the cloudy midafternoon sky.

I hopped right up and tried to block out the cheering from my teammates. Brian jogged back to the huddle.

The next play, it happened again. He rang my bell so hard, his large, powerful thigh crashing into my skull, that I stayed put. I wanted to lie on the ground all day, afternoon turning into evening above my head, sweat and shame drying in the cool autumn wind.

Brian looked down at me, smiling through his own helmet, a grin that told me everything I needed to know. He was bigger than me. Faster. Stronger.

"You all right?" Brian asked, holding out his hand.

"I think so," I said.

"I really fucked you up," he said, pulling me up from the ground. "Twice!"

He gave me a hard pat on the shoulder pads.

"Don't try going low on me again," he warned playfully, backpedaling to the line of scrimmage.

Playing eighth grade football in middle school made me feel like I belonged. When we huddled before every play, we put our arms around each other, planning our next moves together. We won every single game that year and looked poised to continue our local dominance. But in high school, something shifted. It became clear what we'd need to do for success: lift weights, bulk up, get tough, stop having fun, and start getting serious. All the boys around me changed too. They all wanted the same thing, all on the same quest for greatness through physical will and toughness, through brutalizing themselves and their opponents. I knew I'd never last.

I started to gravitate towards the theatre. On stage, I opened my arms to the world, thrust boldly into a spotlight where I truly felt I could be myself. High school became marked for me in those moments, onstage basking under the lights, offstage talking shit with the cast and crew. There was purity in it, I thought at the time, in that space where the hyper-aggression of the football field would never encroach.

Brian and I remained on friendly terms, and for years after that hit, whenever I saw him at a party or shared a joint with him in someone's car, he always reminded me.

"Remember when I lit you up that one time?" he asked, a gleeful smile spread across his face.

I nodded, slightly ashamed, wondering if I'd always feel guilty that I couldn't take a hit. "Yeah," I said, "I remember."

I attended college at a midsized public university in southern Ohio. The whole town seethed with an energy I didn't understand. Fraternity houses lined the avenues that separated campus from the town itself, like a wall. On weekend nights, they were a crucible of activity, drawing everyone towards their debauched parties. No sorority houses were allowed at the school; women interested in Greek life lived in gender-segregated dorms. This inequality contributed to the pulsating I felt everywhere. Since Greek life dominated campus and the frats received outsized attention and resources, the men seemed to dominate as well.

As I look back, I wonder if that seething energy was a result of a deep investment in and codification of toxic masculinity on campus. I no longer know if there is a difference between toxicity and any healthy attributes associated with masculinity. It seems to me that one influences the other. Thousands of my former classmates may have disagreed. Maybe for them the nights of binge drinking, making out in alleys, screaming the cries of the newly adult, are all fond memories of their way from adolescence to the rest of their life. Maybe the energy wasn't gendered; it was just youth. After all, I too was intoxicated by the freedom to get blasted and act recklessly in public. I too waited in lines to binge drink, made out in alleys, screamed the cries of the newly adult. But the main culture of campus unsettled me, the business majors and conservatives, the mindless thrust towards money and stability.

Like in high school, the theatre kids became my people, as well as the interdisciplinary studies majors—those who made and liked art, those who wanted something more from the world. I like to think that was where anyone, of any gender, could find themselves. But I didn't conceive of more than two genders back then, so I honestly don't know. I can say that's where I found myself, along the edges of campus.

But the town was too small. Sooner or later, you always run into what you were fleeing.

It happened on a Friday night my sophomore year. I'd been spending a lot of time that fall at Lesley, Sara, and Josie's apartment. They were the first people I knew to live off-campus, where they could smoke and drink without getting busted.

I was twenty years old. I smoked a pack of cigarettes a day, copious amounts of marijuana. I drank cheap beer when I could find it. I'd had sex on a few occasions. Okay, twice.

I crushed on Lesley. We had met the first weekend of our freshman year of college, walking towards each other on a sun-scorched afternoon, the light dancing between the trees. Emerging from nowhere, it seemed to me then, she asked if I knew where she could buy cigarettes. Petite and funky, she was a laid-back West Virginia girl with long brown hair and a near-constant desire to get high. I didn't know how to make a move, couldn't bridge the friendship gap between us.

That Friday night started off great. It was my friend Andrew and me, Lesley, Josie and her boyfriend, and Sara. We were sitting on the cement pavement outside their apartment. Early 2000s neo-soul played from a boom box. We'd rolled a few joints, downed a couple of beers, no one too loud or unruly. It was everything I wanted: friendship, a little medicine, good vibes.

Until Nat M. strode over the grassy lawn in front of their

apartment. We watched him stumble as he approached, swaying on the uneven ground. I'd met Nat briefly at orientation the year before. He was tall and cut, muscles rippling over his hockey-player arms. I felt tiny in his presence.

"Hey, Nat!" Lesley said, and he walked into the house, slamming the door without saying anything. His entrance, like he owned the place, confirmed something: he was hooking up with Lesley. I felt my face go hot with shame and felt like I'd been wasting my time trying to get her to like me.

When Nat walked inside, eyes straight ahead, muttering under his breath, we all looked at each other, a nervous giggle breaking our chill.

"You okay there, buddy?" Lesley called inside.

That's when all hell broke loose.

I don't know what set him off, what drugs—if any—he'd been using, but Nat blasted out of the apartment in a rage. He picked up a lawn chair and tossed it into the grass, kicked beer bottles, and then shattered them against the side of the house. The girls screamed, "Nat! What are you doing?" Josie's boyfriend, high as a kite, started laughing at the exchange. Nat stalked over to him, pushing him roughly into a car. "You wanna go!? Say somethin'!"

"Nat! Stop it!" Lesley yelled.

Slowed by pot and alcohol, I couldn't really understand what was happening. I felt like I was supposed to get involved, to protect my friends, to subdue Nat in some way. He was on us in a flurry. "Nat! Stop!" the girls yelled again. Andrew was so drunk he was giggling. I was scared and quiet. Nat grabbed both of us by the back of the head—at the same time—and slammed us into the pavement. Andrew used his arms to cushion the blow, but I took the brunt of it with my forehead, bouncing off the cement.

"Nat!" Lesley yelled, with more force than I ever thought to give her credit for, "Stop. It."

He softened then, her words getting to him. Lesley pulled him to the grass, where they conversed quietly.

Sara kneeled down next to me. "Are you okay?" she asked.

I wasn't. I knew I could never protect myself or anyone else if a guy that strong wanted us punished. It wasn't fair, that his brute force dominated everything, that we were all powerless to stop it.

Later, after Nat had gone home, after I'd cleaned up the little bit of blood on my forehead, after I'd applied an ice pack to my whiplashed shoulder, I broke down. I stood in the kitchen and cried. I was embarrassed, worried about how I might've looked to Lesley, but I couldn't help myself.

"I don't do anything to harm anybody," I said, "and I just don't understand why this would happen. Why he would do something like that."

"I know," Sara said. "I don't understand either."

The next day, I went to the health clinic. They gave me muscle relaxers for my neck but didn't ask me about what happened. I spent that night playing video games at my friend Aaron's apartment with some buddies and another guy named Mol, a dude from Aaron's hometown.

When I told them about the night, how a hockey player slammed my forehead onto the pavement, Mol interjected.

"What was his name?"

"Nat M—," I said.

"Nat M— did that to you?" Mol asked, eyes narrowing. He paused the video game and stood up, shaking his head back and forth. "That is unacceptable. I can't have my guys acting like that. It's not how we do things."

"Mol's the captain of the hockey team," Aaron said.

"I'm so sorry that happened to you," Mol said to me. "The violence on the ice stays on the ice. There will be retribution."

Nat was kicked off the team. He had a reputation as a loose cannon, and it came back to haunt him. I remember gloating about it, like I'd won a victory for the little guys.

I spent most of college avoiding guys like him, those brutes

Nicholas Ward

who would pop off at a moment's notice, but perhaps that wasn't the best tactic. I also carried a power in my body, the power to hurt people, to scare them. I might be smaller in stature, but I knew how to make my presence known; I knew how to be heard. In the theatre spaces where I found myself, I know that I talked loudly with no end in sight, that I spoke over people, interrupted, argued, took up space. I never clocked those spaces, those behaviors, as toxic back then, but I know now how much I contributed to an unhealthy culture.

By avoiding Nat, I avoided myself. I didn't try to understand what made me tick, what traits we both shared. Maybe I could have done something. Instead, I fled.

Ten years later, I found myself in Europe. I'd just turned thirty-three years old. In the years after college, I'd moved to Chicago, made a life and career in restaurants, then professional theatre. I'd fallen in and out of love so many times I'd lost count. And I'd quit smoking for good, this time. But after another breakup—a particularly bad one—and after quitting my prestigious job at a renowned theatre company, I'd decided to run to Europe. I felt like I'd made a rubble of my life. And even though before I left Chicago, I met and started dating a new woman—one whom I couldn't wait to see again—I still felt lost. A decade-plus into adulthood, I was still so unsure of who I was and where I was supposed to be. I thought this trip would offer some clarity.

It happened on the last Saturday night of my ninety-day trip. Budapest was alive that night, wedding processions and party buses and exalted cheering rising from the streets. I splurged on a three-course meal at a bistro near my hostel. After a few glasses of wine, I felt good. Comfortable. A little tipsy. My hostel sat on a main road, the restaurant off a side street down from the National Opera House. There were bars and clubs aplenty in the vicinity. It was my last weekend night in Europe for the foreseeable future. Anything could happen.

I paid for the tab and started walking. It was a typical side street, pockets of light on either end but dark in the middle. My mind swirled with the possibilities. I was excited to stay out late, meet people, sleep off a hangover, and spend the last of my money in a hazy flourish. I was so caught up that I barely noticed the encroaching footsteps at my back or the unfamiliar language getting louder in my ears. All of a sudden, he was right in my face.

The man was shorter than me but fierce looking, with a shaved head and gigantic eyes that looked like they would burst from their sockets. He was speaking roughly, Hungarian I assumed, the words exploding from his lips. I don't know what he yelled or why he was screaming it at me. I'd crossed some line I didn't know existed. I froze, no one else on the street, unsure what to do and how to act.

He continued to berate me, and I watched him slip a hand into the pocket of his jeans. I don't know what he was going for, a knife or a gun. I backpedaled, putting my hand out to ward him off. "Whoa, whoa, whoa," I said, on my heels, making back towards the restaurant, where people were still eating. If I got there in time, someone would come to my defense.

After a few paces, the man stopped. "I go this way, you go that way," he said in English, confusing me further because the way he pointed me to go was the exact way I'd been walking.

"Do you want to come in here?" a voice asked over my shoulder. I spun to see a girl with the door to her building half-open.

"No, thanks," I said. The man continued on without looking back. "I don't know what happened. He just got in my face."

"Are you okay?" she asked.

"Yes," I said, not wanting to appear flustered to a stranger. "Just a little freaked out."

It was the weekend of Sziget, a music and arts festival that brings half a million tourists to the Hungarian capital each year. There were people everywhere in the plaza by my hostel. They lounged on the grass, sat at café tables, dipped their toes in the plaza's pool, drank openly from bottles of wine and cans of beer. I watched from the balcony of my empty hostel, quiet on a Saturday night. The flirtation and the festival, the community and laughter, the revelry and adventure. It all left me empty.

I feared my would-be attacker was off in the crowd somewhere, prowling the streets, looking for someone else to harass. Looking for me. Intellectually, I knew this was probably a random occurrence, that he was fed up with tourists in his hometown, or even mistook me for someone I wasn't. Emotionally, I thought it might be a reckoning.

It happened one year earlier, not too long before my trip to Europe.

I was thirty-two years old. I lived with my girlfriend, Dina, in a beautiful apartment in Chicago. I'd poured everything into the relationship and it just wasn't working. It was my third long-term relationship and the second time I'd lived with someone. I was so scared of another failed romance. I didn't want to end up alone.

We'd been dancing around so many issues, Dina and I: our careers, our time spent together and apart, our lives. We both knew we needed to confront each other.

That September night, drunk on wine on our back porch, we finally came to a point.

Dina, curly hair piled dramatically atop her head, was considering pursuing a job opening in a faraway city.

"If you get the job, would you want me to move with you?" I asked. If she said *Yes*, I told myself, we could figure out all the messy details of our life together.

She took a breath. "I don't know."

From somewhere deep and dark inside me, I lifted a biting remark that I knew would crush her. Imagine the worst thing you can say to someone you love, a partner or parent or child. Imagine you can excavate the darkest place of that person, where they feel most insecure and vulnerable. Imagine saying this directly to their face.

Dina sobbed and ran inside.

"Come on!" I shouted and followed her all the way to the front of our apartment, where we kept a spare room for house guests. She tried to shut the door, but I pushed it open and she pushed back. I forced the door open again, something vengeful coursing through me. I don't know what I meant to do; I'm not even sure who I was in that moment, just that I was devastated and terrified and angry.

"Get away from me!" she wailed, tears streaming down her face. I backed away, slamming the door and leaving her to cry alone. I faced our living room, spotting a stack of binders, archives of projects she'd worked on the past few years, painstakingly assembled. I picked up those binders and chucked them, kicking them all over the house, throwing them onto the couch, scattering the pages as far and wide as I could, until I crumpled on the floor. In that moment, I'd become the one thing I hated and feared most in the world.

My understanding of my own gender is constantly evolving so that I'm often wondering how masculinity sits on me. I present like someone our culture historically sees as running a boardroom or working in finance or real estate or politics. I'm worried that being who I am means that I can access the world but that I'm kept from my own humanity. Being stifled in this way doesn't just hurt the women in my life—those I date and love as well as friends and family—it impacts my relationships with other men as well. If there is a block between us and our truest selves, if we can't remember tenderness, care, and compassion, how can we ever truly approach one another with generosity? I wonder now if it is even possible to walk through the world in my body—with all the power and privilege contained therein—and not be infected by unchecked masculinity. It is a sickness. A disease. I'm worried it possesses us all: Brian. Nat. Me.

Sweat

I'm on Van Buren, in the Loop, when a man approaches me. Years later, I will imagine that he watched from afar, following me, seeking out a kindred spirit.

"And how are you tonight?" he asks, sidling up on my left.

I raise an eyebrow but keep walking. "I'm fine," I say. I'm a little drunk and a lot sweaty and my feet stink and I am not in the mood for chitchat with a stranger.

From Grant Park, I can still hear the sounds of Lollapalooza, fading as we walk. The L rumbles over our heads. The scene reminds me of those Chicago movies I watched as a kid—*Ferris Bueller's Day Off*, *The Untouchables*, *The Fugitive*—movies where Chicago looks perfect. For a suspended second, I'm reminded why I live here.

"Do you, uh, know where Berlin is?" he asks. I'm not sure how I know this, but I realize that he's referring to the all-inclusive, give-no-fucks, open-to-all-sexualities club on Belmont.

"I know Berlin," I say. I don't think much of the question until later, when I wonder: why did he ask about Berlin? To discern my sexuality? To see if I was down?

The Harold Washington Library is across the street, the sun rippling over its red bricks, and I direct him to the Red Line, and from there to the club, quietly congratulating myself on passing the test of a true Chicagoan.

But as I cross with the light, towards Dearborn, he's still at my shoulder, keeping pace with me. "No," I say, "you need to go that way, the station's just over there."

"Wait a minute," he says, and I stop, facing him for the first time. He's a white guy, a little shorter than me, a tad older, balding, with spectacles. I'm not sure what to do.

"May I help you?" I ask.

He takes a deep breath. "Don't judge," he pleads.

When I first moved to Chicago, I walked around the city with an analog camera, a small black thing with an internal flash that I thought took good photos. Digital cameras had already conquered the marketplace, but they didn't interest me. I wasn't a photographer. I was a wanderer. I wanted to feel like I was on an adventure, in pursuit of something.

I found the city through that camera, or rather the city I wanted to see at the time, downtown and the North Side. I spent most of my first few years in Chicago wandering around River North, first handing out resumes, then waiting tables at two different restaurants. I adored that neighborhood back then, loft apartment buildings, art galleries slung into basements under the L tracks, elegant restaurants and dirty bars. I took pictures of churches, of street signs and wide avenues, of the Chicago sky. I stole time before evening shifts or extended my afternoons after lunch,

Nicholas Ward

ambling north to the Gold Coast and into Old Town, or back down into the Loop. That's where I made my first collage, standing in one location and taking a series of photos from one panorama to the next, inching my viewfinder along. This was on Michigan Avenue, across from the Congress Hotel. Once the film was developed, I stuck the photos together with tape and glue. I still have that collage, carrying it with me from one apartment to the next.

I wanted to figure out where I lived, to learn my new landscape. It's easy to look back now and wonder about my choice of locations. I didn't stick much to my neighborhood. Logan Square was the place I lived, not where I explored, not where I would build my life. I wish I'd invested more of my time, more of myself, in that neighborhood. With its wide boulevards, sprawling green spaces, and the limestone columns lining the main thoroughfare, the neighborhood—avenue by avenue—is one of the most gorgeous in the whole city. Now that it's fully gentrified, now that bars and restaurants have bloomed from utilitarian storefronts, now that the Megamall has come down, shiny buildings have gone up, and the full transformation of the neighborhood complete, I wish I'd documented the old Logan Square more. I wish I'd captured the neighborhood as I once saw it, new to the city and on fire with my life.

Chicago is now an international palace on the lake, a glistening metropolis with a stately Riverwalk. The furious city development has been made possible by public money siphoned from tax increments funds, from schools closed in Black and brown neighborhoods, from city services privatized. I didn't know anything about how the city operated when I moved here, how Chicago crushes its own people. I wonder now what my life would've been like if I never stopped to question, if I lived my entire existence blissfully unaware, if all I ever did was spend lazy afternoons walking around amongst the skyscrapers.

By the time Lollapalooza moved into Grant Park, I'd lived in Chicago a year. I was twenty-four years old, head completely shaved, in possession of a fantastically vague vision of the person I wanted to become: a gregarious intellectual artist who investigates the mysteries of the universe with like-minded people, preferably over beers. I didn't know how to achieve that. I didn't bond with my coworkers, hadn't taken classes or been in a play, so meeting people proved hard.

I wasn't friendless. But after living with my best friends from college—Will and Betsy and Matt and Stefanie—for a year, after they all got engaged and began planning their lives, I realized that my friends and I were different people. We envisioned opposite lives for ourselves, held separate values sacred, immersed in the culture of the city along parallel avenues. That's okay. It's healthy to cultivate an assorted network: people who are teachers or office workers, who own real estate and start families before they turn thirty, who believe in different gods, who might actually (and I'm serious about this) lean conservative—or at least moderate. At the time, I was devastated to discover that my friends didn't want to share my sacred experiences with me. When I asked them if they wanted to go with me to the first non-touring Lollapalooza in Grant Park, they weren't as excited as I thought they'd be.

"I'm not spending my weekend sweaty and gross and outside, no thank you," said Betsy, camped out on her couch watching *Queer Eye for the Straight Guy* and painting her nails.

"Dude," said Will, sweeping the kitchen floor, "I only get the weekends to spend time with Betsy."

"I listen to country music," said Matt, smoking cigarettes in our backyard with Stefanie.

"We don't know any of those bands," she added.

"You don't know the Pixies?!?" I asked. "I play them all the time."

"Nick," Stefanie said, "nobody in this apartment cares about the Pixies like you do."

Nicholas Ward

I arrive at noon when the park opens and realize I'm one of the first attendees. I drink some beer, eat a hot dog, watch bands by myself, and kick around until three p.m.

I spot a group of eight—six women and two men—lounging under a grove of trees by the rose garden south of Buckingham Fountain, stretched out on the grass. The clock is ticking on the day—if I'm to accomplish anything, it has to happen now. I linger along the periphery of their camp. I don't know how to begin. "Would you like to investigate the mysteries of the universe with me?" might be a little too heavy.

"Hi," I say, affecting a persona like I'm about to tell them the specials at my restaurant. "I'm here by myself, you wanna hang out?"

A white girl in a green dress raises her sunglasses and takes me in. I'm wearing a white shirt already drenched in sweat, cargo shorts, and white socks up to my knees. I want to assure her that I'm not trying to pick her up, that I like girls, but I'm here to meet people generally—but even still, if we connected and then made out later, that'd be cool too.

"Yeah," she says. "I don't really think so."

I try a group of bros in backward baseball caps. I like sports almost as much as I like music; maybe I can connect with them. They wave me along too.

The third time is a charm. "Yeah, sure," a guy with floppy blond hair in a large, amorphous crew of hipsters says, "have a seat."

We make introductions and talk about the festival, who we've seen, who we're excited to see. But after those pleasantries, I make no inroads. They all seem to know each other really well; they have quirks and idiosyncrasies and a group rhythm I don't understand. I could float in their orbit all afternoon, but we're never going to be friends. Not really. I don't know what I was thinking, why I thought I could build a lifetime of connection in a single day.

I watch the Pixies by myself, on a hill overlooking the crowd, the mass of bodies swaying, August sun setting against the Field

Museum. It's stunning, a sea of people, but I can't share this moment with anyone. I snap a picture of the expanse and move on.

I completed the best of my photo collages at Ohio Street Beach, some random weekday afternoon in the summer. I was trying to capture the way the buildings got smaller as the coastline of Lake Michigan opened northward, coalescing into a point somewhere farther north that I rarely ventured. It wasn't until I opened the developed film and began piecing the photos together that I realized what I'd done. In pausing between shots, lining up the images in a precise manner, I'd captured a small girl walking towards the lake in three separate photos. In the first, if I remember correctly, she strides confidently along the sand. By the third frame, she's almost to the water's edge. She wears a T-shirt and shorts, unusual for a child taking a swim. Who is she and where is she going? Is she supervised? Did she escape from a family member's grasp? Is her mother wandering Chicago in a panic, begging anyone who will listen for information about her little angel? Or is she just enjoying a day at the beach before school and homework and house chores render her childhood unbearable?

Looking at the collage for the first time in many years, I see it now: she's not alone. She's running to catch up with her friends. Why did I block them out of my mind for so long? Maybe it's because she reminded me of the self I wanted to be: carefree and alone, independent and strong.

I miss those days, and yet I do not long for their return. I didn't know anybody outside of my college friends and I had no idea how I was going to make it in the city, get involved in its artistic landscape the way I envisioned. And the Chicago I saw was a fiction, a curated playground that overshadowed and overlooked so many on the margins, that reduced my new home to a few square miles—even if it was beautiful to observe.

Nicholas Ward

He takes a deep breath.

"Don't judge," he says, "but if someone were to offer you forty dollars to lick and suck your feet for fifteen minutes, what would you say?"

I stop fidgeting and stare at him.

"I would say no," I say. I don't want to get my feet sucked by this guy—my feet are gross, and I don't care what he likes to do or who he likes to do it with, but no, not me, move along.

"Come on," he says, "it's only a couple of minutes. My place is right around the corner. We don't even have to go in. We can just stay in the hallway. I'll give you the money upfront."

I take a step back, slowly, putting my hand out in front of me like I need to preserve our distance. The guy looks tired. His eyes sag a little behind his glasses, sweat sparkles off his forehead, shoulders stoop. How long has he been talking to people on the street? How many times has he been denied? Does he feel like the world doesn't understand him, like it never will? It occurs to me that we might be mirror images of each other, two lonely men looking for some sort of connection.

He takes a deep breath again; it looks like he's about to cry. "Forty dollars for fifteen minutes," he says. "All you have to do is stand there. Please."

I open my mouth to respond and, in that instant, time crystallizes, and I feel everything so acutely: the L train flashing sparks over our heads, the day's beer gurgling in my belly, the sweat trickling down the crevices of my skin. Let the world judge his advances as weird; I don't care. This is my chance, to share an experience with someone, to boldly throw myself into a new adventure.

"I can't," I say. "I'm sorry." I take a few steps backward, turn on my heels, and then I'm gone, bounding towards the Blue Line, sprinting for the train as it reaches the station, not looking back, not pausing to take a picture.

The Match

It's seventeen days after. I'm sitting on the basement floor, waiting for the phone to ring. My mind plays the last two-and-a-half weeks in an endless loop. My butt presses on the cold linoleum, Dad's Apple 2GS workstation behind me. *Reservoir Dogs* plays on the VHS for the hundredth time, but I'm only vaguely watching. I don't understand. It's Saturday night. I don't have work at the Pasta Stop counter. Summer vacation lingers around the corner. I should be out with friends, I tell myself, not cooped up in front of the TV.

Upstairs, my parents' party sounds the muffled notes of clinking glasses and laughter. The door opens and I hear my mom's footsteps clomping down the stairs.

"I thought you were getting together with Kurt and Ryan

and Jonny tonight," she says. "Have they not called yet?"

I shrug. "I thought they'd call by now but maybe not."

"You could go over there." She's trying to be helpful.

"Mom," I say, with a tone. "I'm not gonna do that. I don't even know where they are."

"Sue me for making a suggestion," she says. "You're always welcome upstairs if you have nothing else to do."

"I know."

I had plans. I thought we had plans. When I saw Kurt and Ryan and Jonny at school yesterday, I told them I didn't work tonight and they should call me if anything is happening, and they said, "Yeah, sure," but they always say "Yeah, sure"; it's basically how they communicate now, all flexed arms and puffed-up chests and angry faces. This is new, this—I'm not even sure what to call it. Macho stuff, I guess. I thought we were still friends, but now it's nine o'clock and they haven't called, and I realize they're not going to.

We had all grown up together, spending summer days at the pool and winter afternoons on the sled hill; each day was spent planning the next. They're my only friends: Kurt, tall and thin with dirty blond hair, who wears baggy jeans with long looping chains, who never seemed to get annoyed when I'd sit in his room and listen to music while everyone hung out downstairs; Ryan, a bulldog with slicked-back black hair, arms always stuffed into his leather jacket, Kurt's real best friend even though Ryan's parents took me with them on vacation to Alabama once; and Jonny, short like me, prone to hemp necklaces and retro bell-bottoms, almost always tapping out some sort of drumbeat on whatever surface was available. We had always lived in a care-free world, one we didn't make but that kept us safe. More than friends, we were brothers. I thought.

It's ten days after. Kurt and I box in his basement. It's more spacious than mine, carpeted and soft, everything shoved into the corners, guitar amp in one, Nintendo in another, punching bag swaying against the wall. We only have one pair of gloves. I took the right hand; Kurt insisted on the left. He thinks he can beat me with his off-hand.

Kurt has shed his jeans and leather jacket, down to green workout shorts and a black A-shirt while we spar. He's bobbing and weaving around me.

"Whatchya gonna do?" he taunts, shimmying his shoulders, bouncing on his feet. Ryan and Jonny are watching from the stairwell, looking bored.

"Kurt, this is dumb. Do we really have to do this?" I'm wearing pleated khakis and an oversized white button-down. Not dressed for boxing.

"Put your hands up, jabroni." I raise them to my face, half-heartedly, but Kurt's still dancing around my feet. "I'm too fast for you, too strong," he says. He throws a quick left, which I block with my right glove, but then his open right hand is inches away from his face, and he gives me a quick tap on the cheek. It doesn't hurt, but I spring into action.

Recently, Kurt's embraced his mother's Italian heritage. We've been watching *Donnie Brasco* on repeat, while he sings the praises of Rocky Marciano and says things like "bafangool" in a weird Brooklyn-y accent. He acts like our leader. A few weeks back, the four of us were in my '94 turquoise Ford Escort, passed down to me by my dad, sitting at a stoplight, and I said, "Hey, Kurt, go fuck you'self" but as a joke, and he spun towards me, finger in my face. "Don't you ever say that to me again, you hear? Show some respect!" I stayed silent. We already did everything he wanted. Wasn't that respect enough?

He taps me on the cheek and it doesn't hurt, but I lose it. Without thinking, I reach my right arm back and clock him in the face. I think it's an accident but I'm not really sure. If Kurt is going to act tough all the time, maybe he deserves to get clocked on occasion.

Kurt hits the floor. He's not out, but he's stunned. A mixture of elation and terror wash over me. I half expect him to come charging. Ryan and Jonny keep staring.

"What the fuck?" Kurt says. "We were just messing around, you don't have to take it so seriously." He stands up. Kurt would find a career in the martial arts, would move to Detroit with the wave of white gentrifiers, would grow a shaggy beard. "This is why no one likes you," he says. "I'm gonna get ice. Don't follow me."

"That was a dick move," Jonny says, bounding up the stairs after Kurt.

I look to Ryan. I've known him the longest. As children, we went everywhere together, to the neighbors' pond to look for frogs, the Maryland coast with my family, the Alabama Gulf Coast with his. Last summer, we shared our first cigarettes under the jungle gym by his house, stubbing them out in the gravel when small children came to play. He's bulked up now, lifting weights at the local gym, no longer the floppy, boisterous kid I knew. I want him to make a joke, to take the piss out of me, like old times. I try to find his eyes, but he won't look at me. He trudges up to the kitchen with our friends.

It's three days after. I wake up in the middle of the night in Jonny's bedroom. Jonny never sleeps over at anyone's house. We'll all be hanging out, intent on passing out in someone's basement after marathon movie sessions, and around midnight or two a.m., he'll get in his car and drive home. Before we could drive, he'd call his mom no matter the hour. Even crashing at his house is unusual. We have to stay in the bedroom, Kurt and Ryan and me in sleeping bags surrounding his wood-framed bed, like sentries protecting their king. It's never all the way dark in that room, incense burning, lava lamps lit. We wonder about this behind his back—why Jonny's afraid of the dark.

Tonight, I wake and hear voices.

"He looked stupid," Kurt says.

"Acting all crazy," I hear Jonny say above me, "like a maniac flying around." I keep my eyes closed. They're talking about me. They're talking about the talent show. Three days ago, we rocked the house in a performance for the ages.

"That song was a joke," Kurt sneers.

"He can't even sing," Jonny says.

"Oh god, the singing," Kurt and Jonny start giggling, shushing each other to keep their voices low.

I don't hear Ryan, so he must be asleep too, or silent.

I freeze in my sleeping bag. If this were Kurt and he found out we were talking about him behind his back, he'd go apeshit. I wish I could rage like that, demand my friends' respect and have them give it to me. But I can't. I take a deep breath in the darkness, tears escaping my eyelids, and keep quiet. If they catch me crying, they catch me listening. Eavesdropping and shedding tears break some code I don't understand.

"I'm never doing that again," Jonny says.

"Well," Kurt says, "never with him."

I get it. We're a crew. Kurt and Ryan and Jonny and Nick. Brothers, I guess. But for five minutes three days ago, I outshone them during the talent show. For a moment, I stood out alone.

It's the day of the show. Usually, the opening and closing numbers are reserved for seniors. But this year, my friends and I, mere sophomores, were awarded the opening slot on the strength of a blistering audition. There are five of us: Kurt on rhythm guitar, hair so spiky you can cut glass on it; Ryan refuses to participate but still hangs in the wings, arms folded; Jonny plays the drums with fresh hemp bracelets and new bell-bottoms; and I'm on lead vocals, Vans on my feet, a blue-and-black checkered shirt, loud purple jacket. On lead guitar is Paul, a friend we've known since way back. We're not really a band. Kurt and Jonny can play, I can kinda sing, but Paulie is our unifying factor. He coached us through rehearsals, gave me singing tips, shredded at the audition.

Nicholas Ward

We're assembled behind the auditorium's thick velvet curtain.
"You nervous?" I ask.
"No," Jonny says, "are you?"
"I'm a little nervous," I whisper.
"Shut up and get focused," Kurt says.
Ryan looks on, arms still folded across his chest.
Off to my right, Paulie stands poised behind his guitar.
The hosts call our names. The lights dim. The curtain rises.
Jonny's drums kickstart us and we fly. I throw myself around like a maniac, belting the lyrics to "Dancing with Myself," tearing off my purple blazer, and hurling the school's microphone into the audience. Our classmates flip their shit. At the front of the stage, I soak it all in, the standing ovation, the catcalls, and high-fives. All for me. For us. When the curtain falls and I turn back to congratulate my friends, my brothers, they've already left the stage.

It's seventeen days after. I'm sitting on the floor of my basement, watching a movie I've seen a hundred times, waiting for a phone call that will never come. I'm replaying all of this in my mind, from the song to the late-night provocations to the match with Kurt last week. Only seventeen days for everything to fall apart.

"What about Paul?" my mom asks as she heads back up the stairs. "Didn't you have fun together at the talent show?"

I think about it. I could call Kurt and Ryan and Jonny, bother their parents, drive around until I locate them, pester them, grovel until they accept me back. Or maybe they'd tell me to go away. Maybe they'd just ignore me. How much more humiliation do I really want to endure?

Or there's Paul.

We've known each other for a long time. After our song, while we were packing up, Paulie said, "You can really wail, man." I smiled, grateful that the coolest kid in school, who knows more about music than I ever will, thought that I'd done a good job.

What I don't know is that Paul and I will form the closest friendship unit I'll ever know, that he'll teach me I can wear nail polish, can listen to Chopin and the Wu-Tang Clan, that we can exist both independently and connected, neither of us leader nor follower. I don't know the effect Paul will have on my life.

I pick up the phone.

The Dresden

Even now, I can see myself standing there on the stoop outside my freshman dorm. My parents had just left: Mom weeping, Dad shepherding her off to drive back to Michigan and an empty home. On the quad in front of Dennison Hall, students fluttered to and fro, caught up in our new life, hurtling towards a trajectory we couldn't yet understand. Certain my parents were long gone, I stuffed a Parliament Light in my mouth and sparked it. I ran my hand through my hair. I used too much gel, but I wouldn't know that until much, much later.

It was a shining late summer afternoon in southern Ohio. A guy with cowboy boots and hair down past his shoulders sat on the stoop next to me. He remembered me from our theatre school auditions. His name was Will.

"I am really looking forward to smoking whenever I want," he said, lighting up a Winston. "And not just at the gas station."

"What gas station?" I asked.

"BP in Steubenville," he said. "Home of Dean Martin and Big Red Football." I should note here that Will no longer claims the football community in his hometown with much pride—not after the name of his town became synonymous with rape culture. "I changed oil, pumped gas, worked the register."

"You smoke weed?" I asked.

"I don't like it," Will said. Like many things, that would change.

Kids and their parents continued to move in around us. A shorter guy sat down.

"You got a light?" he asked, Camel Light perched in his lips. I tossed him mine.

We sat down on the concrete slabs, far enough apart to not get too close.

"I'm Matt," he said, "I'm from Lakewood, just outside Cleveland. St. Ed's High School."

I shrugged.

"Catholic School. Good football program."

"I never had a friend who went to Catholic School," I said.

"Why not?" he asked.

"I didn't really like any of them that much."

Matt leaned back, took a pull. He smiled. "Maybe you'll like me."

"You guys have a good football program, right?" Will asked.

"One of the best," Matt said. "Never can seem to beat St. Ignatius. You play?"

"I was in the band." Will said. "First trombone."

"The band?" Matt asked.

"We're in theatre," I said.

Matt seemed perplexed. "The first two guys I meet are actors," he said, grinning. "I play rugby."

"Didn't know we did that in this country," I said.

I had no idea what we were talking about. Or why. But I

guessed the easiest way to make friends was to trade our bona fides and see how they landed.

Will and Matt and I became fast friends, grafting on to each other out of proximity and luck, fortressing ourselves together in our new existence. It seemed to us, back then, that we were so different from one another, a private school rugby player and two public-education-championing theatre kids.

It was the fall of *Stankonia* and Bush v. Gore. It was the fall I got cast as the lead in the main stage play. It was the fall my friends and I realized how we related to the other boys on campus.

For freshmen commencement, a few days after that stoop meeting, we ambled through the north side of campus to the basketball arena. On Tallawanda Road, the boys from Sigma Nu greeted all the first years walking by. They drank beer in tank tops and shorts, blasting "The Freshmen" by The Verve Pipe, a ham-fisted breakup song that was nevertheless designed to intimidate us.

"Hey, Will," I said.

"Yeah," he said, as we walked past, the frat brothers jeering at us. They sat on cinder blocks, cases of Natty Light at their feet. They cupped hands around their mouths, calling out to the girls in our promenade.

And even though I had just met Will, I felt confident telling him: "Let's never become that."

"We're not joining a frat," he said. "So, we never will."

By senior year, I just wanted to get the fuck out of town. One night during the final week of college, Will and Matt and I decided to get more trashed than we'd ever been in our lives. We called it Blackout Wednesday, and we had one goal. Though we'd never joined a fraternity—well, Matt had but claimed to never pay his dues—we'd spent four years drinking and smoking our way through school. It seemed a fitting capper for the whole affair. Much of campus was hunkered down studying for finals, but we were seniors with few classes. I didn't think of myself as lucky, but as a theatre kid with sights set on acting in Chicago, I wondered if I even needed to be there.

The location for Blackout Wednesday was Matt's front porch, and the recipe was simple:

Step 1. Smoke a bowl.

Step 2. Drink a 40 ounce of malt liquor. Preferably Olde English but Mickey's would suffice.

Step 3. Smoke another bowl.

Step 4. Go out drinking. Uptown, the strip of bars up the hill from where we lived, would be dead. We'd have the run of the place.

Step 5. See what happens.

It was the spring after *Speakerboxxx/The Love Below*, the Bush v. Kerry election a few months away, and debates raged throughout town over who was better. Most people I knew picked the straight-ahead rap of Big Boi, but we preferred the weirdness of Andre 3000, the way he funneled Prince and Funkadelic into his own version of R&B.

That night, we needed rock 'n' roll, that full-throttle release. The Darkness, popular at the time, played out of this crappy stereo resting in the corner of the patio, one of those cheap '90s jobs with the two speakers connected to the main receiver. We adored their hit song, especially the part where the singer wails, "I believe in a thing called looovvvvvvvvvveee / Ooooooooh / Guitar!" and the solo blasts in, and we always air-guitared like we were on some arena rock stage. But that night, just as our end-of-college, gettin'-fucked-up fest was cresting, just after Step 3 in our plan, the song got to "Guitar!" and the stereo stopped working.

"What???!!!??!" we all yelled, our shouting reverberating throughout the neighborhood. That section of town, a four-street rectangular indentation, was nicknamed "The Ghetto" for the consistently poor quality of houses that kids in our school chose to inhabit. My house had once probably been a garage with no installation. Will's place, just across a soggy patch of grass, should've been condemned. As for the name, well, maybe we knew its racial coding and didn't speak of it. Or maybe we claimed the name for ourselves, like so many other white kids trying on aesthetics that weren't theirs. Either way, I realize now how easy it was to inherit the name from previous generations and pass it along unchallenged.

Matt inspected the speaker. "The fuck happened?" he said.

"I think it's dead," Will said. "Probably why Caroline gave it to us." Matt's roommate had plopped the speaker down outside at the beginning of the night and asked if we wanted to use it.

"What the fuck are we gonna do now?" Matt asked.

Will swooped down to pick it up, holding the mainframe away from his body like he was going to throw it into the street.

"Dude, don't do that," I said.

"Why not? It's not like we need it anymore."

"Just wait." An idea came to me, a devious plan, something dangerous and powerful, something I realized at once I'd wanted to do for many years, to purge the whole place from me. "By the time this night is over . . . we're going to throw it through the window of The Dresden."

Our sophomore year, we secured a corner suite in a dorm on the north side of campus, near the basketball arena and frat row. Matt and I took one room while Will bunked with Rance—Matt's high school classmate—in the other. "Suite" makes it seems a lot gaudier than it was, two small rooms with bunk beds and a tiny entranceway. Often, we turned on the shower and got high in the cramped bathroom or blew the pungent weed smoke through a "blow-tube" made from a used toilet paper roll stuffed with dryer sheets. We smoked cigarettes constantly; I'd climb to the top bunk each evening with a thin layer of smoke hanging over my head.

One night, early in the year, I woke to all the lights turned on and Matt keening over the side of the wastebasket.

"Are you okay?"

"I don't feel so good," he said, more of a moan than a sentence.

"What's wrong?"

"I was hooking up with Jemma,"—a rugby player who lived down the hall—"and . . . I think she gave me blue balls."

"Blue balls?" I asked. I was only vaguely aware of what that meant.

"I'm in so much pain," he said. "Can you call 911?"

"For blue balls?" I asked. We were, at this point, used to Matt's antics, but I'd never seen him like this.

"Yes. Please."

I hopped down from the bunk and dialed 911.

"What's your emergency?" a woman asked. She sounded thrilled to be talking to me.

"My roommate is in a lot of pain," I said. "I think he needs to go to the hospital."

"What kind of pain?" she asked.

"He says . . . um . . . he says he has blue balls."

"Blue balls?"

"Yes, it's when—"

"I'm familiar with the term, sir."

"Can you help?" I asked. "Please."

She sent a cop, and we piled into his cruiser on the way to McCullough-Hyde Hospital. We got Matt settled, and I promised to visit him in the morning.

I walked back home through the north side of town, a mash-up of apartment buildings, small bungalows, large houses. It was late, past two, maybe three in the morning, on a Monday. Classes had just started a week before. I realized I couldn't remember the last time I'd been awake that late and sober. I'd never experienced the town that quiet. I kind of liked it.

Around eleven the next morning, the dorm phone woke me

up. It was Matt, calling from the hospital.

"Turn on the television," he said.

"Why?" I asked. "Are you okay?"

"Kidney stones. Turn on the television. Planes flew into the World Trade Center and the Pentagon."

"They give you some good drugs in there?" I asked.

"Just do it," he said.

In the aftermath—and one could argue that we're still living in the aftermath—of 9/11, there was a spread of something toxic, of misinformation and fear. We heard a Muslim student had been beaten up on campus; a friend of mine from high school signed up for the Marines; there were endless conversations in our theatre classes about what it meant and what the country would do in response. One night, as we walked past a large party on our way home, the whole crowd was singing—in unison—that song, "Proud to Be an American," with aplomb and not a hint of irony. It sent shivers down my spine and bothered me in a way that I couldn't quite articulate at the moment. I understand now how bothered I was by patriotic rhetoric, how embarrassing I found it. I didn't have a choice of where I was born. Did I really have to love my accidental nation-state?

I buried my interests elsewhere. The Strokes' first album was released, and I was drawn to its apolitical swagger, bopping down the walkways of campus with my Discman at my hip. And I fell in love.

I don't recall even meeting Lindsay. One minute, she was a friend of a friend of a friend, and the next, we were talking all day, every day on AIM via the campus's ethernet connection—still a novelty in the post-dial up days.

Honestly, I don't remember much about her now. She was a hippie; we smoked cigarettes; she loved music and talking about music, she was a former figure skater, and she was—like me—from an affluent suburb outside a big city and deeply uncomfortable with what this affluence meant, without trying to alter it.

I just remember what it felt like to crush on her: a spine-tingling sensation that today would be the day that I'd reveal my true feelings, and we'd ride off into the sunset together. But I had no idea how to love her, no idea how to turn my crush into action. So, we smoked and we took mushrooms and we went to parties where I watched her fall in love with another boy, thinking it was only a matter of time before she chose me.

One night, after the winter and into the spring, we all ambled over to a party at Mike Long's house. Mike was a senior in the theatre program. He wore Baja hoodies almost constantly and promised parties with "free beer and hot girls." A bunch of us went: Matt and Lindsay and Rance, Will's new girlfriend, Betsy, and more kids from the theatre department.

That was my first night at The Dresden. A house on the north side of town just two blocks from Matt's eventual senior year front porch, The Dresden represented a typical Oxford, Ohio phenomenon: large off-campus houses featuring names and accompanying signs, but they weren't fraternities or sororities. They weren't for families. They were close to campus and the bars, housing anywhere between four and fourteen college coeds. There was "No Class"; there was "Deez Nuts"; there was "The Dresden." A large clapboard construction, The Dresden was set back from the road ten feet farther than its neighbors with a wide lawn in front used for beer pong or cornhole. Inside the house lived twelve of the biggest dickheads in the history of mankind. They were the boys who got other people to steal lunch money. They boasted about that chick they banged last night. They manage hedge funds now, but they don't own them, and they never will. As guys graduated and moved out of the dorms, the boys rolled over every year—a wave of new recruits.

It was a typical college party—kegs, flip cup, Nelly on the stereo. We milled around out front, warm enough in the early spring.

"Hey, Mike," Will asked. "Why'd you guys name this place

Nicholas Ward

The Dresden?"

Mike took a sip from his beer, wiped away a strand of his floppy, curly hair. A sly smirk spread across his face. He leaned in. "We were gonna get a sign that said 'Bend 'Em and Spread 'Em,'" he said, "but that's, you know, not appropriate. Even if it is true."

Matt and Will and I exchanged uneasy glances. Mike looked pleased with himself. I was grateful that Lindsay was in the house, elsewhere.

He continued, about how the name took inspiration from the movie *Swingers*, how they go to The Dresden in Los Angeles at the end, but I wasn't listening. My head spun. I knew Mike could be a sleaze—he'd never let up talking about how attractive the girls were in our department—but I was shocked to discover who he really was. I wish I could've harnessed everything I felt in that moment, the anger and frustration and outrage, and channeled it into a devastating, soul-destroying, Tony-Award-winning monologue. I would have stopped the whole party: "*You! You are unacceptable to me! Because I stand for love and decency and tolerance, and you and all the men of your house represent everything I stand against! And from this time on, we are enemies, you and I.*"

Instead, I trotted off to get another beer. I didn't want to disrupt a good time.

Lindsay asked me to walk her home. As we cut down the Slant Walk onto campus, past the arches where it was said if you kissed someone, they would become your spouse, she eased her hand into mine. A shot coursed through my body, pulsating with electricity.

"Oh, Nick," she said. "You're my best friend."

I swallowed hard, the electricity fizzling. I don't know what I said, and I don't know if she noticed my hurt. I didn't want to live in a world in which we were just friends. I hadn't even seen this being the outcome.

It was a lonely walk home that night, weaving through a darkened campus. When I got back to the dorm, all my buddies were there, and I raged, letting it all out. I slammed my open hands onto the frame of the bunk bed, threw pillows around, screamed loud enough to wake up the whole quad. When Matt tried to comfort me by putting his arms around me, I wheeled on him: "You don't understand! I'm in love with her!"

I wanted to know why it couldn't be me. Why all the campus dickheads were the ones who floated through the world with so much success. Why all the boys on campus, from the popped-collared frat guys to the ironic interdisciplinary studies majors to the stoner hippies, the hockey and football players, were all the same, a bunch of fucking dickheads.

After years of living around people like that—years spent in dorm rooms and classrooms and libraries and bars and on porches and in houses and apartments surrounded by idiots, years of Will and Matt and I saying, "Those people are dickheads," "We should totally do something," "Yeah"—after four years of *that*, we'd had enough. I'd had enough. If nobody else was going to step up, we would.

Later that Blackout Wednesday, we stood in the backyard of The Dresden. Hidden in that small cluster of trees, we stared up at that clapboard siding, at the windows of the back bedroom next to the kitchen. A party raged in the front of the house, but everything was calm and silent in the backyard. Will and Matt each held a speaker, and I held the main unit of Caroline's broken stereo. We'd achieved Step 5 in our night of partying. None of us thought this was a bad idea.

"You guys ready?" I asked.

"Yep," they said.

"All right. One ... two ... three." We heaved that stereo at The Dresden, and it collided with those windows and absolutely shattered them.

"Run!" Will screamed. We tore off across the street. Matt slipped and fell in the middle of the road, but Will and I didn't stop. We got to the other side, slowed to a run-walk, and ducked into a nearby house party. We moved through the party swiftly and deliberately, past the guys playing pool and the girls shaking it to Jay-Z, through the beer-soaked kitchen, out the back door, and into the night. We shuffled stealthily for two blocks behind people's houses and then circled back around to Matt's front porch.

"Where is he?" I yelled. "Did he get caught?"

"Shut up," Will said. "He'll be fine."

Five minutes later, Matt showed up, panting and out of breath. "I fell in the street and went the other way. I can't believe we just did that."

We were silenced by police sirens, faint and distant. We sat on the porch and watched as four cop cars, lights blazing, descended on The Dresden.

Will raised his arms in disbelief and held them a moment. No one said anything. That weekend, we graduated from college.

A few days later, after graduation weekend, Will and Matt and I were sitting on that front porch again when Caroline and her boyfriend, Dave, returned home from brunch with parents.

"Did you hear about The Dresden?" they asked.

"No," we said.

"Some people threw a stereo into the house," Dave said, "glass everywhere, windows totally destroyed. But the guys at The Dresden found 'em. Beat the shit out of them."

"That sucks," Matt said, trying to put on a neutral face, but I could feel the information weighing on him. It weighed on me too.

Caroline and Dave went inside to pack, and we stayed on the front porch. We were silent for a long time. I never knew if Caroline figured it out, putting the pieces together over where her busted stereo ended up that night.

We didn't speak much the rest of the afternoon. I don't know if we ever imagined what would happen if we got caught. I don't think we expected to. Even now, I can see us all sitting there, smoking cigarettes, on a beautiful afternoon in southern Ohio. It's only by looking back that I can see us so clearly: in the end, we realized we were just like all those other boys too.

No
Honest
Way
To
Make
a Living

Mid-America's Finest

I stared at the soups. They'd been congealing all day, deep pans hissing away in their steamer tray. Burnt edges lined the sides. I pulled two of the white bean soup trays and set them on the counter. ·

"Chad," I asked our kitchen manager, calling over my shoulder, towards the grill line, "combine or toss?"

"Combine," he said, not looking up from the grill.

Across from me, Hilary closed the dessert station, plastic-wrapping our "world-famous" chocolate cake.

"Cigarette?" I asked her.

"Duh," she said.

"Arrion," I called to the fry cook, who stood near Chad. "Drop chicken and fries?"

Nicholas Ward

"Drop 'em yourself," Arrion said, with the same flatness he'd had in English class when I'd asked him if he could score me weed.

I watched Matt and Brad serve the last guests, bickering while they shut down the coffee station. Chimes clanked, another two-top walking in. Evelyn was gone for the night, so they rock-paper-scissored for the table. Brad lost on the third try. Matt danced a jig.

Angel, Chad's right hand at the grill station, tapped me on the shoulder. He still wore the fishnet cap that kept his black hair in place. In high school, he ran with the goths—a senior when I was a freshman—and scared me a little. "For the last time," he slipped my paycheck out of my back pocket, "fold this up."

I shrugged. "They'd have to figure out how to cash it without my signature."

He grinned. "There are ways."

For two years in high school, on evenings and weekends and during the summer, I waited tables at Bill Knapp's, a family diner-style restaurant chain that could be found in Michigan, Ohio, Indiana, and Florida during the '90s. This branch was just up the street from my subdivision. At the time I worked there, I thought I was just passing through, earning cash for gas and other indulgences before I moved on to college, to my real life. But after two decades spent waiting tables, I still remember my first restaurant: what it looked like, how it smelled, the food we served, my coworkers, and how we might have tried to pass the time.

After the shift, we'd congregate over cigarettes and fried food in the break room, a pair of unused diner tables off the dish pit. The servers counted their tips, a strange practice in front of the cooks and dishwashers, who never made more than their hourly allotment.

If it was just me and Hilary, I'd ask about her kids.

"They're the best thing to ever happen to me," she said once, face brightening.

I remembered when she was the prettiest girl in middle school. I remembered when she disappeared from the hallways in high school. I remember thinking that if the best thing to ever happen to her was her family, she was right: what was the point of school?

"When do you leave?" Arrion asked that night.

"Two weeks," I replied.

"Excited?"

"A little." I was bursting with anticipation about college in Ohio, but I tried to remain cool. I didn't know what Arrion's prospects were.

Brad and Matt came back, the guests all gone. They nibbled our food and lit their smokes.

"Rolling tonight?" Hilary asked.

"Of course," Matt said, brushing his shaggy hair from his face.

"It's summer," Brad said, by way of explanation. The rest of the crew waited in someone's nearby garage.

"How many pills?" I asked.

"Two," Brad said, his mischievous smile framed a chipped tooth. "Always two."

They were the ringleaders, older than the rest, the high schoolers, recent grads, drop-outs.

"Wanna come?" Brad asked.

"He's partying with us tomorrow," Matt said.

Brad winked at me. "Tomorrow then."

"I told my parents I wanted to hang with you one last time before I left," I said.

"Aw, that's cute." It was Chad, cigarette perched in his mouth, Angel behind him.

"Cash outs," Chad said. We thrust our receipts and owed cash into his palms. "Now get the fuck outta here." He didn't mean it. Chad's face may have seen a few fights, but he was pretty relaxed. His girlfriend, Judy, one of the floor managers, was as uptight as Chad was loose.

I could have dashed off to a party, where all my high school friends embodied slight variations on the same theme—similar hairstyle and background and soon-to-be colleges. Often, I'd rather sit in the back break area and talk shit with my coworkers over greasy food and cigarettes. It was where I felt I could truly be myself, unhindered from any social pressures, or even my own ambition. A fair amount of my work friends were kids who attended my high school but who I never spoke to before working together. We moved in different circles at school, but at Knapp's, we were together. Work pushed me to get to know them more than was ever possible in school.

We dispersed eventually, Brad and Matt and Angel to their party, Hilary to her young family, Chad to Judy, Arrion to Detroit proper. I went home, across Grand River Avenue and into my subdivision. In the driveway, after my parents went to sleep, I smoked more cigarettes and imagined what it would be like when I left my home and never came back.

The very first Bill Knapp's restaurant opened in Battle Creek, Michigan, in the 1940s, a hundred miles west of my hometown of Farmington. Billing itself "Mid-America's Finest," the offerings were common for the era—chicken and biscuits, white bean soup, Mom's Meatloaf. At the height of the franchise, food was made from scratch in three commissaries and shipped off to sixty-nine restaurants in Michigan, Ohio, Indiana, and Florida. Every Bill Knapp's looked more or less the same, a New England-style colonial with a T-shaped dining room and a friendly matron ringing up checks on a vintage cash register.

As a kid, I looked forward to lunch there with my grandfather. The children's menu organized items by animal; I liked "The Elephant," a chicken fricassee. There was always chocolate cake at the end. Gooey with a rich layer of frosting, the dessert became Bill Knapp's calling card. As I got older, I realized the only people who went to Bill Knapp's were families with grandparents. I thought it was pretty uncool, and I couldn't understand how anyone worked there.

Until I did myself.

I came to Bill Knapp's after a year working at the Pasta Stop, a fast-food counter next to the Baskin-Robbins in my hometown's quaint downtown. Each week, I portioned and cooked vats of noodles. When guests came in, I heated the noodles in boiling water, slathered them with sauce, and slid them down on a tray with breadsticks.

My father had decided it was time I got a job, to get out of the house and learn some hard-working American values. I didn't need to work. I was a middle-class only child; I didn't have to help with bills or rent. My parents had promised to pay for college. My dad even passed down his '94 turquoise Ford Escort to me once I turned sixteen. With the car came gas money and the desire for cash to blow while driving, bored, around the suburbs. I was vaguely aware that I was lucky, but I didn't quite realize how special it was to have parents with stable incomes, to only have to work for fun money.

I hated the Pasta Stop. The stench of the place permeated my skin. The owner popped in a few times a month to criticize our work methods. The fast-casual Italian concept failed to draw a crowd.

A guy from my high school told me he was making double the money waiting tables at Knapp's, and they were hiring. While my friends idled at the local video store or Subway, I started making some real cash. Not that I knew what to do with it. Not that I listened when I was told I should save it. If I'd had to pay bills and rent and car insurance, I would have barely gotten by on what I made. But it was more money than I'd ever seen in my life, and it was hand-delivered each night in cash. Plus, a paycheck every two weeks with a little bit more. It was money that I alone earned, money that I alone was responsible for, money that I could slap down and say, "this is mine."

On my last Saturday morning, Angel and I rolled in around ten o'clock to open. I opted to set up the salad station, which involved

Nicholas Ward

"making coleslaw." Two large plastic bags arrived in a set, one with julienned carrots and cabbage, the other a neon-yellow dressing. We didn't have mixing bowls, so we cut a slit in the top of the dressing bag, poured it into the slaw, and gave a few hearty shakes. Flecks of yellow material splashed on my bright blue shirt.

Chad called over from the line. "You look like you vomited on yourself."

I shrugged. "I won't need this anymore."

"You'll miss us," Angel said, still up from last night's party.

Each week, the same single diners waited at the front door or sat in their cars in the parking lot until we opened. They were older men with tufts of wispy, white hair. They clutched coupons cut from the local paper, thin slips offering three-course meals for $5.99. Evelyn, the lead hostess, called each man by name as she helped them to their table.

By noon, we hummed. Young hostesses rushed to set up high chairs. Waiters ferried large trays of food across three dining rooms. Evelyn sprinted back and forth between the door and the register. She approached her job with rigor. I wondered what it must have been like, working with people so much younger than her. With her hair in a beehive and glasses attached via a chain around her neck, she looked like she stepped out of a bygone era. I can't imagine the old men coming back each week if it wasn't for her.

One day, early on in my Knapp's tenure, I took a to-go order. It was every server's responsibility from time to time, and no one wanted it. The woman stressed to me that I shouldn't forget her order of peas. We always forgot her order of peas, so I needed to make sure I didn't. "Yes, ma'am, of course, I understand."

I forgot her order of peas.

She called the manager, Judy, in a rage. Judy came up to me, terse.

"Why did you forget that woman's order of peas?"

Mistakes happen in restaurants all the time. It's a chaotic, stressful, high-stakes environment. Instead of apologizing, I snapped.

"You know what, I don't care!" I shouted. I was standing in the back hallway where we kept the high chairs. My voice was loud enough to be heard in the dining room.

Judy snapped. "Your attitude sucks," she said. "Go home and cool off." She wasn't that much older than me, now that I think about it, twenty-two or twenty-three.

Knapp's may have been an after-school job, but I wanted to do it well—better than anybody else. When I made mistakes, I lost my temper. It took me a long while not to lose my cool, long after I left Bill Knapp's and well into my professional career as a server. But one thing I did learn in the time I spent at Knapp's was how to subsume the job into my body, until I felt like an athlete in the zone.

That outburst was almost two years before my last shift, and by that final Saturday, I bopped around, grooving to the music while battling away the chaos.

"More crayons for your son who ate them? Absolutely!"

"A seventy-seven-cent tip in dimes and pennies? Scoop that up!"

"Why, yes, Mom is back there making her very own meatloaf. You want some?"

"And what can I bring for you both today?" I asked a booth of two men.

"Um," the younger one, my father's age, squinted at his coupon. "White bean soup, steak medium well, baked potato, and broccoli, and chocolate cake, I guess."

"And for you?" I asked the man opposite him, still wearing his coat indoors, his mouth hanging open. He raised his eyes in my direction.

"Fiddler on the roof!" he shouted.

"What?" I asked.

"Dad," the son leaned across the table and tried to grab his father's hand. "Dad! What do you want? Steak? Meatloaf?"

"Fiddler on the roof!"

Nicholas Ward

I wanted to laugh, imagining a thirty-year-old musical rattling around in his brain. But I could hear the ding from the kitchen announcing a pick-up and one table needed water and another wanted their check. I didn't have time to linger with these two, last day or not.

"Dad?" the son asked again.

The father put his head low, leaned over the retro countertop, and vomited on the table. His son tried to push away as the chunks threatened to spill over onto the carpeting. I stepped back. "Is everything, uh . . ."

"I'll take care of this." It was Judy, at my side with a taut smile and a handful of dish rags. "I understand we had a little accident," she said to the table. She was never that soft with the staff, but I could see in that moment how much Judy cared for our guests.

I spun on my heels, off to a new task.

A few minutes later, while scooping bean soup into two bowls, Judy found me. "They're good, they're going to try to eat," she said.

"Thank you," I said. "I didn't want to clean that up."

"It's your last day," she said. "Otherwise, I would've pushed your nose in it."

I smiled. Angel was right: I'd miss this place.

By 1998, when I started working there, Bill Knapp's had been sold to a California-based conglomerate. The new corporate overlords rolled out a rebranding campaign called "That was then, this is WOW." Select franchises installed flat-screen TVs, video game consoles, pumped extra-loud rock 'n' roll through the speakers, and painted the interior an array of fuchsias, turquoises, and purples. They even removed certain staples from the menu. Our store in Farmington didn't receive the upgrade, but Livonia did, and we siphoned off their business. Families with young kids couldn't dine with all that racket. Teenagers sensed the pandering a mile away. Their core clientele, those solo diners who arrived by rote ritual, moved on.

No one asked us, the servers or managers, what we thought. No one really got a chance to know the customers. No one arrived at the store on a weekend morning in the winter to watch the quiet-but-earnest exchange between guest and worker.

When we envision the American waiter or waitress, who do we think of? Maybe an overly cheery, plump woman at a roadside diner who calls the guests "hun"? Or a pretentious suit-jacketed man opening and pouring a bottle of wine? Or perhaps we think of the person that I was for most of my serving career: a young artist trying to balance paying rent and pursuing the dreams that don't make them enough money to live? In truth, we are all of those things and none of them. We are young and old, cynical and idealistic, students and drop-outs and graduates and doctors, with families and pets and mortgages and bills.

In 1998, almost two million people worked as servers in this country. On average, they made twelve grand a year—about nineteen thousand in today's dollars. That's not really enough to live on, to buy groceries and make car payments and pay rent, then or now. Most servers are subject to firing at a moment's notice, products of at-will employment. Most of them don't get asked about big decisions at their restaurant. Most of them just grind away.

As the divide between the haves and the have-nots widens in this country, between executives who make the decisions and the underpaid workers who carry them out, I think about my first restaurant job with rose-tinted nostalgia. It seemed to me then that we were all in it together, responsible for making something special for our guests, for taking care of each other when we needed to. But maybe that's bullshit too. Maybe we were just people, working for ourselves and our families, exploited by corporate America.

After that final Saturday shift, I joined Matt and Brad and the rest of their crew for one of their raves. They used to roll every weekend, sometimes both Friday and Saturday. Often, over the course of two years, they asked me if I wanted to join them. I always demurred. I was no prude: I drank, got high often, smoked cigarettes constantly. But the amount of partying they did surprised me. Their ecstasy use felt like a step too far, even when they explained that they were young, that they worked hard, that they'd earned it. I also worried I'd get too attached to those people, not just my friends but everyone in the sprawling scene, that I'd love them and their lifestyle too much to walk away. But finally, I relented. One night couldn't hurt.

Before the party, standing in someone's garage, Brad handed me two pills.

"Lots of water," Matt said. "You might feel nausea. I feel it too."

"Don't take them both at once," Brad said.

"That's important," Matt said, stabbing the air with his cigarette. "Take the second a few hours after the first."

Brad gave me a shoulder pat. "Just stay close."

The party was in the woods off I-96. Matt's beat-up sedan pulled onto a gravel road, through a thicket of trees. We stopped at a clearing. Spotlights shone on a barn. Young kids directed us to park on a bedding of hay. Inside, DJs spun techno, kids danced with glow sticks, and people wore bright colors and baggy pants. We fanned out. I took the first pill. Nothing happened. I took the second pill. That feeling Matt described, the nausea sensation, bubbled to the surface, and I couldn't control it, so when no one was looking, I vomited onto a tractor in the corner of the barn.

That's when the drugs kicked in.

I felt light. Airy. Speedy. I needed swift movement. There was a beat. I started dancing by myself, in a little circle, kicking my legs and popping my arms. Someone offered me Special K, but I didn't need anything else, just the music and the lights and a place to dance.

Suddenly, the music cut. The lights came on. I stopped spinning. Everyone scattered, trying to get out before they got caught. I scanned the barn. I couldn't see anyone. Bodies moved around me. Where had they all gone? Matt grabbed me.

"We're here," he said, face emerging from the chaos. Brad stood just beyond him. It never occurred to me that they could leave me, though I guess that it might have been possible. Somehow, I just knew that they'd take care of me, make sure I was safe.

We filed outside. Maybe I should have been more concerned about police activity ruining the rest of my life, but I knew they had nothing on me, that they couldn't see the drugs in my system. All I was doing wrong was trespassing.

It didn't look like the cops were arresting people, just checking every car for drugs.

"Sit in front with me," Matt said.

"Are you okay to drive?" I asked once we got past the police.

"Yeah," he said, as he eased out onto the main road. "I drive better like this." I had to believe him. I didn't have a choice.

It started to rain as we merged onto the highway. Matt leaned forward to see, his shitty windshield wipers ineffectual.

"Don't worry," he said. "I got this."

And he did. I arrived home safely the next day. A few weeks later, I went off to college. It would be convenient to claim that I felt a great reawakening inside myself, that the culmination of my work life and my first hard drug experience lifted me into a greater plane of clarity from which to view my life. In the moment, though, I just wanted to get home safe, sleep, and leave. I have only now begun to look back.

"That was then, this is WOW" failed so spectacularly that they purchased local radio ads years later, apologizing to their guests and announcing a return to the old decor, menu, and aesthetic. But the damage had been done. Bill Knapp's closed all their stores in one fell swoop in 2002. I heard everyone showed up for work that morning, but the doors of the restaurant had been padlocked.

I was in college in southern Ohio, surrounded by cornfields and sky. I'd begun working at a small fine-dining bistro in town. I wore a pressed white shirt and tie and learned about wine and service. In some ways, it was better job training than I received at the university, since I would move to Chicago and find a life in restaurants.

When I heard news of the closing, I thought about my old coworkers, about Hilary, with two kids by nineteen; about Judy and Chad, who had built careers in the company; about Matt and Brad and the rest of their crew, working doubles to roll on the weekends. I thought about Evelyn and the old men she greeted each Saturday morning. I don't know what happened to any of them.

I know now that I never really belonged to Bill Knapp's, that I was both within and without, and that it was my fault for being in that position. I'd spend my whole life in restaurants like this, feeling like I never expected to be there in the first place. I sometimes wonder if that means I denigrated my colleagues, that I placed distance between us. I assumed I was just passing through, from one version of my life to the next. At the beginning, I never imagined that the restaurant life would get under my skin and stay there forever. I feel guilt about my past assumptions. I feel like I missed opportunities to get to know my old colleagues on a deeper level, to follow the trajectory of their lives, to find communion the further we got away from our jobs. And I wish I had gone to more of their parties.

A new restaurant never replaced Bill Knapp's on that stretch of Grand River Avenue, where the apartment complexes meet the highway, where the shopping mall got torn down and replaced by a sleek, glass building inconsistent with its previous land use. When I travel to my parents' house, I always peek at the land of my first real job. Now, a medical group shares space with a dentist's office. The new building is closer to the road; the façade is polished and bland. But it's the same A-frame colonial design, holding some shadow of the past. I wonder if anybody else remembers it. If they drive by and pull in, looking for chicken fricassee and chocolate cake. If they recall that after-work smoke with almost-friends. If they search in vain for something that used to be.

Nacional 27

It was the night before Christmas at the Bar Louie on Chicago Avenue. Even on a good night, the bar felt lonely. Bar Louie is long gone, like almost every other bar and restaurant from that era of my time in Chicago, replaced by an upscale gastropub. That night, morning really, Jeff, Luis, and I should have gone home after our shift at Nacional—we all worked at Nacional 27, a fine-dining restaurant around the corner from Bar Louie—but we needed a drink, wanted to raise a glass to the end of the year and the end of something else.

"What time is your train tomorrow?" Luis asked. He would celebrate with his roommates, whom he knew from Ecuador, many of whom worked in the industry.

"Six a.m.," I said. I flipped open my phone to check the time.

"Five hours from now."

"Let's have another," Jeff said. He signaled to the bartender, who slumped over the prep table, talking to the grill guy. Jeff's family lived downstate, halfway between Springfield and St. Louis, closer than I lived to my parents' house outside Detroit, but he wouldn't go home either. He just didn't want to.

"Your last night is next week?" Luis asked.

"New Year's Eve," I said, "out with a bang."

"You nervous?" Jeff asked.

I shrugged, a deflection.

Another round of beers arrived, and we toasted in the Chicago way: raise the glass in your friends' direction, tap it lightly on the bar top, take a pull. Jeff and Luis were the first non-college friends I'd made, the first of that sort to last.

"You can't do both?" Luis asked.

"It seems too hard," I said, "requesting off so many nights, closing when I have auditions the next morning. If I'm going to take my life seriously, I might as well do it now."

"I don't get it," Luis said.

"It's a career move," Jeff said. "I'm proud of you."

"Thank you." I said, taunting Luis. "At least someone understands me."

For Christmas Eve comida, the pre-service staff meal, one of the sous chefs, Gustavo, cooked roasted plantains, rice and beans, and extra suckling pig we'd acquired for dinner service. Everyone ate together before the shift, all the cooks and bussers and bartenders and food runners and hosts and servers, congregated around the long circular bar as the day faded to dusk.

We weren't busy that night, slow enough that I still remember my guests. One was a woman and her younger brother. He tried to order a drink. When I asked for ID, she asked, "You can't make an exception, just for tonight?"

"Wish I could," I said.

Nicholas Ward

I placed her drink between the both of them, knowing that when they shared it, I'd look the other way. I wondered if their parents were alive, if they were making new rituals. I wondered about my own parents, what they'd say if they knew I'd asked to work this lonesome, miserable shift, helping other people celebrate.

"The guy is back," Jeff said. We stood at the entrance to the dining room, a circle of plush, black booths with tables in the center and a raised platform beyond. On a busy Saturday, the room exploded with heat. That shift felt cold.

"Dead wife guy?" I asked. Jeff nodded. I looked across the room, at the guest Jeff served earlier in the week. He was seated at the same four-top, an empty place setting in front of him. A few days before, another slow pre-holiday night, a host of personnel had tried to remove the extra setting, but he insisted it stay. He told Jeff that his wife had just passed away and that he wanted to keep the place for her.

"It's your table," Jeff said. He handed me a chit from the host stand, with the man's name and a note in all caps: LEAVE ONE EXTRA SETTING.

I sighed. "Today must be really hard for him."

"Tomorrow is gonna be worse," Jeff said.

I stumbled over to greet him. I can no longer remember what he looked like, what he ordered, if I offered my condolences. All I recall is that as I approached him with a strange loping gait, I realized that I'd split my pants. Because I was leaving the job, I hadn't bothered with uniform maintenance and had allowed a tiny hole in the taint region of my black dress pants to elongate until I was forced to walk with clenched buttocks. The sole of my right shoe was nearly detached and flapped on the tiled floor.

After work, I tried to use my wardrobe malfunctions as an excuse not to go out. I was downstairs putting on my overcoat when Luis cornered me in the break area.

"Beers?" he asked. He leaned on the door of the locker room. He looked like a model with his coiffed, black hair.

"I have an early train," I said.

"You don't need to be sober for that," he said. A fair argument.

"Man, my pants are split from ass to cock and my fucking shoe has a hole in it."

"No one cares," he said. "We need to make use of our time together."

I relented, like he knew I would. "Is anything even open?" I asked.

I'd begun working at Nacional 27, on the corner of Huron and Orleans streets, in the winter of 2004. An upscale restaurant that turned into a nightclub on the weekend, the place enthralled me. A large ad for the restaurant had been painted on the side of the building, a seven-story office space visible from the Brown Line, depicting a woman's leg protruding from her nightgown in mid-dance. The image had been plastered directly onto the bricks, so that some of the bricks themselves poked thru the off-white and muted pastel green. It gave the appearance of something worn and nostalgic. Inside, cream-colored curtains nestled the free-standing bar with liquor bottles stacked to the ceiling. It looked how I imagined a Havana nightclub might have before Castro: opulent, pulsating, a playground but only for those who could afford it. I knew family diners, sports bars, national chains, and white tablecloths for special occasions. Nacional was in a different solar system.

I interviewed twice, in two different rounds of job searches. "Why do you want to work here so badly?" Jay, the manager, asked me on my second interview, after I'd spent a few months at the old Cy's Crabhouse on Ashland Avenue.

"Look around," I said. "This place is sexy. I want to be a part of that."

In college, I worked at a small bed-and-breakfast called The Alexander House. It was high-end for a college town. We free-poured drinks and served chops with a minimum amount of plating. The chef offered some adventurous forays: a calamari fritto misto, a lavash cracker for flatbreads. Like most of the staff, I was often in some state of dishevelment: hungover or un-showered or surly. Most times all three. In Chicago, and at Nacional 27, I started to take the craft of working in a restaurant seriously.

Colorful and vibrant, the menu mixed spicy and savory and sweet in an array of flavors. There were plantain croquettes, tiny BBQ lamb tacos, ahi tuna and watermelon ceviche, shrimp adobado, tender pork confit, and beef tenderloin medallions topped with a chimichurri crust. The wine list boasted hundreds of bottles, 27 of them under $27, the big boys topping out at $300. I drank malbec and carménère and petit verdot for the first time. The cocktail program spun classics like mojitos, caipirinhas, and pisco sours, alongside inventions like El Corazón—tequila with pomegranate and a hint of spice on the rim.

We didn't serve chips and guacamole. "We're not a Mexican restaurant," Chef Randy said. "There's nothing wrong with chips and guac, but we're concerned with everything south of North America." Bald with thin-framed spectacles, Randy Zweiban was from Queens but had spent decades under the famed Florida chef, Norman Van Aken, who cooked what he called "New World cuisine," a mash-up of Latin, Caribbean, Asian, American, and African flavors. Van Aken claimed to have invented the idea of "fusion food." Randy worked in the Nuevo Latino tradition, a different but related cuisine. The guiding principle was that the United States had smashed together the people of the Caribbean and Central and South America, and that they had naturally begun to exchange cultures and flavors with one another. We saw ourselves as advocates of this cuisine and delivered the news with aplomb. How amazing that Nicaraguan people ended up in Omaha. How delightful to project the sun-caked images of *The Motorcycle Diaries* on the wall. How delicious the food that came from all of that struggle.

Looking back on it now, that positive and ultimately capitalist spin makes me cringe. Explaining our cuisine through the lens of colonialism, imperialism, the transatlantic slave trade, Native American genocide, CIA-backed assassinations, and neoliberal U.S. policy wouldn't exactly excite our guests to indulge, but all that knowledge I have now is hard to accept. Randy loved the food he cooked and the people who helped inspire it. His leadership kept Nacional singular, even though he never learned Spanish. Indeed, when Randy finally left to start his own restaurant, the corporate overlords at Lettuce Entertain You, the conglomerate that owned the restaurant, put chips and guac on the menu, opened a section of the restaurant as a taco stand, and never hired another executive chef. I didn't keep my eyes on how business went over time, but after the coronavirus pandemic in 2020, Nacional 27 closed for good.

By the time I started working at Nacional, I'd lived in Chicago for four months. That time felt endless to me: four months of wandering, working a job I hated, four months of waiting, always waiting, for my life to start. Nacional changed that in an instant. Suddenly, I was on fire with what the world had to offer. My first night on the floor, after two weeks of training, I got along so well with my final table that, when I saw them across the street at the Green Door Tavern, they bought me a drink to celebrate my first successful night as a fine-dining server in the city of Chicago.

Luis started a few months after I did, in February. He was tense. He sought a life in restaurants and connected his future success with this first opportunity in a fine-dining Lettuce Entertain You restaurant. Such was the power of the group: once you were in, you were golden forever. Anxiety clouded Luis' judgment, wrecked his ability to learn and translate the menu to his guests, and disrupted his grace under pressure. One of his first nights, he ran afoul of Randy. It was a busy Saturday,

Nicholas Ward

and he'd screwed up a bunch of orders. Randy pulled Jay and the other manager aside and told them he wanted Luis fired. The managers pivoted, sent Luis home, and told him to come back the next night knowing the menu front to back. They tasked me with taking over the tables in his section. "You saved my career," Luis once said to me, much later. I waved the compliment away. "No, you did," he said. "If you didn't take my section, I'd get fired, and who knows where I'd be today." Luis studied the menu and aced his test. Eventually, he became a manager at Nacional 27, hired me twice at different restaurants, and is now the Director of Operations for a gigantic conglomerate in Denver.

Luis drove everywhere. My roommates and I had access to cars, but we always took the train if we could help it. Not Luis. After work, we'd climb into his VW Bug and zip to his favorite bars in the city. Luis favored dumb sports bars in bland neighborhoods. He didn't even like sports. He never blended into bro culture, but his favorite bar was a slab-of-concrete hellhole near his apartment in Lakeview called Tai's Til 4. We'd stumble in after two o'clock, drunk but coherent, and watch blackout-types fall over each other. I wondered about the bartenders, what kind of debauchery they witnessed on a nightly basis, what the bar looked like after all the drunks left, vomit and piss and sexual fluids all over the place.

One Saturday night in the summer, the new guy at Nacional, Jeff, with funky hair that shot straight up from his head and hung in place, joined us for a night out. When offered a ride, he declined, saying instead that he'd brought his bike along. "You bike that far?" I asked, outside a bar in Lincoln Park. Jeff nodded his head. "It's not that far," he said. When we pulled up to Tai's and piled out, there he was, pulling up to the curb. Jeff was the first person I knew to ride a bike in Chicago, an activity I now prefer as my main mode of transit. A few nights later, I was humming a song while making coffee in the kitchen. Jeff cruised past me on a different mission. "Tom Waits?" he asked.

"It is," I said. "You like Tom Waits?" ,

"I love him."

That sealed our friendship. Jeff was a music obsessive, and we bonded over the latest releases. It felt good to have a friend like this, someone with whom I could share my interests. Towards the end of the holidays, Jeff gave me a mix CD with his favorite songs from that year.

We three became inseparable, in the restaurant and out. We pounded beers after work at the Green Door Tavern across the street, followed Luis to his favorite shitholes. The night the White Sox made the World Series, we blew our whole take on a fancy dinner at Smith *&* Wollensky, overlooking the Chicago River. A few days later, when Jeff's beloved Astros did too, I joined him for celebration drinks.

Working at Nacional created an internal tension I lived with for years. I'd moved to Chicago to be an actor. I told myself to audition at a fever pitch, to really go after my acting life with all the tenacity I could muster. But at Nacional, I found a vital space where I could meet people, make friends, learn about food and wine, and make more money than I ever thought possible. Each night on the floor was its own mini-play, with servers and managers and runners and bussers and bartenders who dazzled the audience, with a whole host of craftspeople backstage, pulling levers the crowd didn't know existed. I loved the action and the rituals that held it all together.

Each shift, the whole staff ate together at Table 81, the semi-private round table up the ramp from the DJ booth, reserved for large parties. Over comida, we'd talk shit—mostly at each other, sometimes about the guests we had last night, the just-okay restaurant we went to the week before, or just bullshit about the weather, politics, sports, movies. Speaking a mixture of English and Spanish, our shit-talking was vulgar and offensive, an HR department's nightmare. "Hola, pinche Nick," Jesús, one of the bussers, would sing. Once finished eating, pre-shift started, the time for the chef and managers to run through the night's activities, talk about specials or important guests; occasionally, they'd offer tips sent down from corporate. We always hated those, some suit trying to tell us how to upsell a few additional sides to boost our check and the corporation's coffers. I liked the time between pre-shift and the start of dinner service, each server and busser assigned daily tasks: folding napkins, stocking plates and glasses, polishing the silverware until it sparkled just so. The tasks were tedious but critical. If we couldn't finish them before the guests piled in, the night could go down in flames.

By far the best part of the job, of any serving job, was talking to the guests. Nacional started me on a path of loving food, of trying to understand food. Pushing that excitement out into the world was easy. Over time, I learned how to read a table: to guide guests that really wanted suggestions, to back off from those who needed space, to change my inflection based on their energy, to know when to push them toward that extra drink. I learned how to describe our restaurant with tenderness and vitality, to showcase its sexiness. I learned that a good server is a tour guide and a magician, that they spin guests through the experience and anticipate their needs without them even knowing what they wanted. When they leave happy, intoxicated, and love-drunk, having spent money they didn't even know they had, and waving away their concerns for a few hours, with an extra thank you on top of that big fat tip, that was the real action.

Every Friday and Saturday at 11 p.m., the entire restaurant transformed. Tables were whisked away from the center of the dining room, the large centerpiece containing stacks of carefully inlaid glasses and trays of silverware wheeled off to an undisclosed location, and suddenly, we had a dance floor. The bar swelled with an influx of people: regulars who came each week to our club and new arrivals curious about our Latin beats. Each week, the same song kicked us off, a booming bass thundered from the speakers, and we coalesced into a very hot, very sweaty, and often-packed Chicago nightclub.

These transitions exhausted me. If I closed, i.e., worked the nightclub after my serving shift, I became a cocktail waiter, ferrying trays of drinks back and forth. But the pathway from the bar to the dance floor was often blocked, so most nights I'd have to go all the way around, into one door of the kitchen and out the other side. Drinks took twenty minutes to land at the guests' tables, something they were never happy about. It was loud and sweaty, and the guests were boorish. So far removed from the tenderness of the place just one hour prior. And since I was trying to get my acting career off the ground, it wasn't uncommon to work until three in the morning with a nine o'clock audition. If I didn't have an audition, I'd probably stay up until five or six, and then my whole precious Sunday was shot.

One night, Jesús dropped an entire tray's worth of glasses he'd just cleared from a nine-top. It was during the transition, while throngs of people attempted to pass from the bar to the club.

He had maybe packed it too full, which was understandable. He wanted to get it all out of the way ASAP. Shattered glass covered the floor; some staff rushed over to help clean it up, others making space to do so safely. "Who's going to pay for my dry cleaning?" a white guy, slacks and a striped shirt, asked. I spun around on him. "Fuck your dry cleaning, we need to make sure this is safe." He protested. "Go to the host stand. Get a card from the manager." Many nights I was like this, combative with guests and sometimes my coworkers. I coiled myself in anxiety and anger and felt like I needed the release of four to six beers and a cab ride home. I hadn't yet learned to let the muck of the job roll off my back.

In hindsight, it wasn't the restaurant. I couldn't figure out my relationship to my own life. I wanted the thrill of the job and I wanted to pursue my dreams and I didn't think I could have it both ways. I got it into my head that I couldn't maintain a relationship with this restaurant, any restaurant, and still have a theatre career. At the time, theatre was all I wanted. It's worth asking myself why Nacional 27, and the restaurant life, wasn't enough. I had a good job, surrounded by people I enjoyed, in pursuit of something we all made together. As I got older, I learned to appreciate that solidity. But back then, I needed more.

I announced my departure from Nacional one night in early December. I was in the office, turning in my cash-out on my way out the door.

"Jay," I said, with a dramatic sweep of a hand. "I need to give two weeks. I just got too much theatre stuff going." I concluded with a deft bow. If I expected a ticker-tape parade, Jay shrugged. "Sounds good," he said. "How's New Year's Eve for your last night?"

I wasn't being offered the moon. I'd just completed the run of a play, a small storefront Shakespeare production. Another company, a bigger one, wanted my services as an understudy, which I assumed was a huge honor (it wasn't). I auditioned at every opportunity. I thought I was approaching the precipice, that moment when I would step from one life into the next, from the heady boyhood days of working in restaurants to the grand life of the stage. I didn't believe that I was destined for greatness, only that I was ready to take the next step. But now I know: there is no final "next step," not if you're an artist, or hell, even if you're after a career in restaurants. If that's your life's path, you have in front of you a series of small triumphs, near misses, Pyrrhic victories, soft regrets, and failures that might look like success.

"Where shall we go?" Luis asked. We stood outside Nacional's revolving doors. It had begun to rain lightly, turning soft snow into slush. I wiggled my toes. They were a little wet already.

We looked at The Green Door Tavern, closed for the night.

Built, they say, on the rubble of the Chicago fire, with a slanted roof to prove it, Green Door was our favorite bar. That's where we wanted to drink, but we were happy for Paulie and his crew to be closed early for a holiday.

"Blue Frog?" Jeff suggested.

"You think there's gonna be karaoke tonight?" Luis asked.

"You never know," Jeff said.

We set off, the streets of the neighborhood quiet. The Brown Line rumbled over our heads. It was still shy of eleven, but the town felt deserted, like we'd stumbled into the pre-dawn.

"Luis, you don't have a hat?" I asked.

He pointed to his black hair, short and swooping across his head. "You think I want to ruin this with a hat?" he asked.

At the Blue Frog, now defunct, closed by developers like most of the great bars in Chicago, Jeff ran to the front door, off the street a few paces.

"How's your foot?" Luis asked.

"Squishy," I said. "I need a drink to warm up."

We watched Jeff peer into the bar's windows. No lights were on.

"You're gonna temp?" Luis asked.

"That's the plan," I said.

"You have experience in an office?" he asked.

"Nope," I said, and we both laughed.

"They're closed," Jeff said. "Clark Street?"

This was 2005, mind you. We couldn't pull out our smart phones and check to see if they were open or even pull up their numbers and call them. We trudged on, past the flower shop on LaSalle, where if you look south, you can see all the way to the Chicago Board of Trade, towards the Clark Street Ale House, fine purveyors of high-alcohol beers. They were closed too.

"I'm calling it a night," I said.

Luis and Jeff protested.

"Noooo, come on, we gotta buy you a drink."

"Guys, I'm tired, my foot is soaked, my pants are split, and I can barely walk."

Luis held up a finger. "One more," he said. "We'll try one more." It wasn't a question.

We turned west on Chicago Avenue, almost completing a loop around the neighborhood. The wide street glistened in the rain, the garish lights of the gas station hazy, cars hissing as they drove the wet streets, maybe to home, maybe to somewhere we couldn't fathom, somewhere they, too, could pretend it wasn't a sacred night.

"The dead wife guy say anything to you?" Jeff asked.

"No," I said. "I was too nervous to talk to him. I didn't know what to say."

"You gotta have empathy," Luis said.

"I have empathy," I said. "But he's not my dad or my cousin or anything."

"You still need to have empathy," Luis said. "That's the job. You have to really care about someone and their life and the experience that you want them to have, and then try really, really hard to make that experience memorable for them, even if you never see them again."

We were quiet. Something about the lights, the sounds of the cars, my squishy foot, the banter with my two friends, talk of death, of finding a beer to drink the night before Christmas, I knew I would carry that night with me.

"Bar Louie?" I asked. We'd stopped across the street, near the entrance to the L. The bar chain's sign was lit up, a few candles flickering in the window.

"I hate that place," Jeff said.

"Me too," Luis said.

"Well, it's the only spot open, so if you want a beer, let's get a beer," I said.

We looked at each other, shrugged our shoulders, and scampered across the street in the rain.

Vong's Thai Kitchen

"Are we cutting anyone?" Rory asked at our pre-shift meeting before lunch, while we ate breakfast and rolled napkins. "I'll go home if we do," he said. Unlike me, Rory also worked nights; he was forced into lunches due to his lack of seniority. Night shifts were where you made the most money, but I preferred lunches as it kept my schedule open for auditions.

"We're not busy," I said. I'd peeked at Open Table when I walked in.

"But we might be," our manager, Danika, said, as she walked up the steps to the private dining room, open for lunch service, and plopped her binder of notes on table eleven.

We groaned. "We might be busy" is the restaurant manager's greatest weapon. If she cut staff and we got busy and couldn't

85

handle it, Danika would hear it from her boss and her boss's boss and, if bad enough, her boss's boss's boss. It didn't matter that we could always handle it. Danika was barely out of college and new to her position; even if she knew we were right, she just didn't have that kind of power. Customers came first. Labor was cheap enough that an extra server wouldn't break the bank. Our arguments fell on deaf ears. Our needs came last.

I was hired to work five lunches, Monday through Friday, at Vong's Thai Kitchen in Chicago's River North. In the beginning, the job was perfect for me. Located within a cross section of shopping, hotels, offices, and landmarks, lunches bustled. Everyone ate at VTK: businessmen, famous chefs, families of all ethnicities, tourists wandering around. I found a rhythm slinging pad thais and Thai iced teas, finished with our famous desserts: mini versions of molten chocolate cake and passion fruit soufflé. If everything hit just right, I could clear sixty to seventy bucks a shift, enough to cover rent in my cheap apartment. My (unpaid) artistic life flourished: I understudied a play, linked up with a storytelling community that would become my artistic home, and followed that with a lead role in another (terrible) play, which was good experience.

But working lunches as my only source of income was a squeeze—any small dip in tips set me back, and restaurants can't predict guests' behavior from day-to-day. The only recourse was to appeal to management to cut servers for that shift, in hopes of letting those remaining servers wait on more tables.

Half past noon, the shift hadn't picked up. Rory and I started in again, begging Danika to cut Rory so I could take over his station. We cornered her at the POS station in the kitchen. It was tucked away from the dining room; we knew that Danika couldn't stand there for very long with no other managers on the floor.

"Nick, how many tables do you have right now?" she asked.

"Just three and two are almost finished," I said.

"I only have two," Rory said over my shoulder.

"Okay, fine, Rory, you're cut, I'll see you at dinner. Nick, take over his station."

"Thank you!"

After quitting Nacional 27, I tried temping, but the work didn't come fast enough. I'd squirreled away some money, but that had quickly dwindled.

One morning, six weeks into my tenure at VTK, I walked in to find all of the managers working. That was unusual. Often, only one of three managers would work a lunch shift, the others flexing for a mid-shift dinner rush and close.

But that day, they'd provided every kitchen worker a paid morning off. The bussers and food runners too. And the guys who worked the dish pit, scraping plates and restacking them for service.

It was March 2006, and numerous immigration rallies were scheduled in Grant Park, kicking off a season of protests, an announcement to the country and the world that Mexican immigrants and others from the Caribbean, Africa, and Central and South America, were as much a part of the fabric of American life as the white men making too many of the decisions.

Danika corralled the serving staff. She explained that she and Sarah would work the floor, helping with bussing and running. Oliver would staff the line with the three kitchen managers, who were immigrants too, rising from lower levels in the hierarchy of the corporate restaurant world. Servers washed dishes. Everyone needed to pitch in. "It goes without saying, but I'm going to say it anyway: no one is getting cut early. Don't even ask. I don't want to hear any grumbling today." We didn't protest.

It was a good shift, nothing we couldn't handle. The food came out more or less on time. Everyone helped each other. The guests couldn't tell that three-quarters of the staff was gone. It would be a long time before I became aware of the systems of power that uphold racial capitalism. Knowing what I know now, the restaurant's closure that day looks like nothing more than a cursory gesture. Allowing their work force to attend one rally did nothing to challenge the status quo, nothing to irk the big business that undergirds most restaurants, nothing to change the power the corporate office had over their employees. After all, they could still fire an underpaid worker at a moment's notice. No one who dined at VTK that day even realized the difference. No one, including the staff who stayed, was forced to confront or consider what the protests were about. I even lauded the restaurant for taking what I thought was a bold stand. We were all grateful when the next day arrived and we could get back to business as usual.

However, business as usual meant the constant tension, and constant tension meant fighting over cutting lunch servers, a fight that I always lost. Losing that fight meant I wasn't making enough money. Dinner presented different problems: rehearsals and meetings and tech and auditions required mountains of nights off, all of which needed approval from the scheduling manager. I knew how hard this would be. I didn't want to get sucked into that maelstrom, but I had no choice. I needed the money that dinner provided. With reluctance, and a little shame that I had just left a lucrative nighttime gig, I joined the dinnertime crew.

As she prepared one of those daikon and carrot salads that we offered guests, a woman turned to me and said, with Minnesota-nice demeanor, "My name is Gretel. I'm a bitch until I get to know you, but then I'm sweet as pie." It was my first night shift.

Though I would come to know her fine qualities, her relentlessness, her loyalty, Gretel presided over the dinner-serving staff with an emperor's hand. She wasn't a manager, and she wasn't assigned any actual status as a lead server. She was a teacher by day at a public school on the West Side and often worked four to five nights a week at the restaurant. A normal person clawing away at life. Nevertheless, a flick of her wrist, a thumbs up or down, decided one's social fate. Rory had run afoul of her at some point and quit.

Gretel and I were similar: white, public school- and college-educated Midwesterners who'd found our lives in Chicago. In fact, most servers I worked with throughout my years were like us, although the wait staff was often much more diverse than every other sector of the business, particularly upper-level management. The restaurant industry in Chicago, like the city itself, is still deeply segregated. In most kitchens, especially at casual, corporate spots like VTK, the line cooks' and dishwashers' roles are often occupied by Latino men; this is the same for the bussers and the food-running staff. At certain fine-dining estab-lishments, the kitchen crew might be white recent culinary school graduates. Management—both front and back of house —was often white, though many kitchens had at least one Spanish-speaking member on their team to communicate to the line and dishwashing crew in a language the chefs didn't speak.

The serving staff, at nearly every single restaurant I worked, was at least two-thirds white. After twenty years of working in restaurants in Chicago, Michigan, and Ohio, I can count on my fingers and toes the number of Black servers I've worked with. The old adage about the restaurant industry, that it's a home for people without college degrees, for wayward souls in need of reclamation, that apparently doesn't exist for Black people.

In some ways, VTK felt different. Bobie, the head trainer, was first-generation Laotian American, who would come in every few days and talk about a boy who'd stolen her heart at some nightclub. Felix was a Black man from the South Side, who sang arias and R&B while we set up for service. Mariana, a Jamaican American woman, shared my last name. Often, while in line for the POS machine, we'd make inappropriate jokes regarding our supposed familial relations. Rafael, from Guatemala, was the eldest server and a PhD student in economics. It was him I sought out one night after I'd received a cash tip that could choke a horse. I asked him what he thought I should do. "Put it in your locker," he said. "Make sure no one else sees it. Take it home immediately."

In other ways, we were not unique. The bussing, running, and kitchen staff were all Latino men, every single one. I don't recall them as well as I do my serving and bartending colleagues. This is partially due to the military-style hierarchy imposed on almost all restaurants since the days of Escoffier, the most famous nineteenth-century French chef. As front-of-house workers, the bus and running staff were technically below the serving staff: we instructed them in their duties and tipped them òut. There had to be resentment. No one likes feeling beneath anyone else. So, we didn't interact in the same way, didn't carouse over drinks after work. I remember the two Eduardos, the dinnertime food runners, one reserved and collected, the other gregarious and friendly, who would describe the food at the table like he was making love to it. I remember a busser named Richard, a high school kid who argued with me about basketball. I remember that one night I worked a private party with Michael, an Ecuadorian American who sold paintings on the side. As we were leaving with the rest of the crew to get beers, we realized that we'd left Hector, our busser, to clean up the entire private dining room by himself. I peeled off fifteen bucks from my take. "Give him thirty for the trouble?" I said to Michael. "Yeah, that's a good idea," he said.

A part of me wants to believe that putting people from different backgrounds together to work on a common cause has value. It's certainly influenced my worldview. But I also can't help but wonder if that's only been a net benefit to people like me. The restaurant industry chews up and spits out immigrant workers. It values their bodies but not their hearts or minds or dreams. One only needs to look at a list of the top chefs each year, the ones who earn Michelin stars, or James Beard Awards, or are provided with the investment capital to open their first, second, and third restaurants, to find out who this industry rewards.

I don't know what it's like walking into a job each day that's presided over and maintained by a white supremacist power structure. Well, I do, and this exists in every industry, but those structures aren't out to get me and often benefit me. I don't know what it's like to have to justify my existence to anyone, and it's pretty clear that mixing people together without equitable payment structures or avenues to advancements isn't real justice. Not even close.

Another complicated facet of restaurant culture includes the prevalence of sexual tensions that can explode a healthy work environment. The comings and goings of sexually active people in their twenties often lent itself to a time-honored cliché and, at VTK, I engaged in several relationships that went well beyond coworker. I first became involved with Larisa. She was glamorous, the kind of woman who, always running late, could slap on makeup last minute at pre-shift and still look stunning. A graduating senior at the School of the Art Institute, she drove a white stick shift pickup truck, which she tried to teach me one night. She moved toward me, flirting during our shifts, revealing surprising details about her life while we were working on the floor, admitting to a hurt that I alone, I told myself, could see.

One night, she came into the restaurant for dinner. I'd been working at VTK for a year and was itching to move on. I stood at the host stand when, on her way out, Larisa stopped to talk to me. We both had awful viruses, snotty noses, sweaty brows, puffy eyes. I shouldn't have been working, but I rarely let sickness get in the way of my shifts. She inched close to me and whispered, "What are you doing later?"

"Chicken soup," I said. "You?"

"Chicken soup with me?" she asked.

"Chicken soup sleepover," I confirmed.

Nicholas Ward

She came over. We did have chicken soup. We kissed. Our fevers broke that night, in between bouts of coughing and holding each other close. We spent almost every day together for two months.

I wasn't ready for Larisa, for her power, for her tender heart. I wasn't ready for nonexclusive dating; in my world view, once you started dating someone, you only dated each other. But she mentioned she wanted nonmonogamy, so I went along with it. Until one night, when Michael was playing blues at Rosa's Lounge, Larisa showed up with one of her other partners. He was older, more our parents' generation, really put together and slick—and rich, I would find out later. "If that's what you want," I said to her the next day, "you're not going to find it here."

"I just want you to be happy," she said.

"You don't get to decide that," I said.

Stacey was another server on staff who grew up in the Detroit suburbs around the same time as me. She and I shared a certain feeling; we called it "the wildness," an incurable chaos that lived inside us. It was a longing, a desire to push it all to the hedonistic limit, full maximum, or as maximum as we were willing to go and still wake up in the morning, still work our shifts at VTK.

After my relationship with Larisa ended, Stacey and I were out one night, stoking that wildness in the kitchen of someone's house. Stacey had fallen down at the bar, and her hip bone was bruised and tender. We kissed in the kitchen while everyone partied in the other room. We spent the night together, that night and a few others. One night, I got beyond drunk and called her eight times to get her to come over, and volleyed a flurry of texts as well. I sent her a message of apology the next day, which she deflected. I learned later she'd been trying the same tactic, drunk dialing and texting to hook up, with a buddy of mine.

Before we started hanging out, Stacey's heart had been busted open by one of my neighbors, Karl, who lived on the ground floor.

One afternoon, Gretel dropped me off at my house, and I saw a young woman moving boxes into or out of Karl's apartment.

"Shit, I didn't know I had new neighbors," I said from the backseat.

When Stacey gave me a hug goodbye, she gave me a look I didn't recognize, a disappointed frown. The woman moving in was Karl's new girlfriend, obvious to me now, though I was oblivious at the time. If I'd been paying more attention to my friend, I would have known. Later that afternoon, while Gretel and I were waiting for our friends to join us for dinner, she said, "Nick, I love you, but if you make a crack like that again to Stacey, I will physically harm you."

Stacey and Larisa and I weren't the only ones adjusting the boundaries of appropriate work behavior. After a male server's marriage broke up, he and another woman server publicly began dating—I preferred keeping everything a secret, if I could—before they fell apart. The singer-songwriter, who crashed with me when his own relationship was torn asunder, harbored a massive crush on Larisa's best friend but eventually dated another coworker. I think they might still be together. One night, while Misty, a theatre kid like myself, was waiting for a ride after a closing shift, she caught Marcus, the bartender, and one of our young woman managers (there were many) in a compromised position. It wasn't long before the whole crew knew. Marcus was a real piece of shit. His girlfriend would sit at the bar sometimes and, when he didn't want her to listen, he'd say, "earmuffs," in reference to the film *Old School*, where Vince Vaughn's character allows people to curse around his child as long as they say "earmuffs" first. Marcus treated his girlfriend like a child. But hell, even I tried to hook up with the manager once, just to see if I could, just to test my own power, to find out if there really were any boundaries that prevented an explosive messiness. I was lonely and horny and thought that "the wildness" was a badge of honor I could wear and not a display of my own internalized sexism. It shows how much respect I had for her position as my boss. She swiftly ushered me out of her basement apartment.

My very last evening working at VTK, we all went to Sing Sing Karaoke off California and Granville, in a strip mall in some part of the city I didn't know existed. It was the kind of joint with rooms you could rent out for the night and ring a buzzer for more alcohol. Misty pushed me down onto the couch and sang "I Touch Myself" by the Divinyls as a going-away present. Later, when Gretel was driving us all home with the sun coming up, Misty texted me from the opposite side of the car: "Let me know if you'd like to go further than that. I can really set worlds on fire." The brazenness of the message shocked me. I never responded.

Tensions were always fraught between the serving staff and the management. Servers felt like they were being asked to work too much for not enough money. We felt like we were being underestimated as a staff, like we weren't being given opportunities to succeed. Management felt like the guests should always come first. Servers felt like we were one of the best crews in town, but we were only making half what other servers made in the neighborhood. We didn't want VTK to raise prices, as that would have risked alienating a core clientele. We wanted to wait on more tables but could rarely get the management to agree. We knew we could all work together and really make the restaurant hum. We never got them to see it our way.

One night, a manager from the corporate office worked the floor. This happened when they wanted to observe, though it was always couched in "helping out," a gesture of goodwill and not a surveillance tactic. This woman, whose name escapes me, had short, curly brown hair with glasses. She pulled me aside after taking a table's order.

"This would have been an appropriate time to upsell," she said. She tried to be polite, but that shit didn't work on me. I snapped at her.

"They wanted pad thais and to get the fuck outta here."

She didn't drop it. "You could have suggested they start with our calamari, or push them towards one of our mocktails."

"Oh, come on," I said, "I know how to read a table. Don't tell me how to do my job." It's pretty shocking that I didn't get fired for that comment and for my well-documented cursing. I didn't have respect for anyone in power in that organization, but I wonder if I knew instinctually if I could snap at her and not the lead partner, who was a man.

I wish I had been better. Gentler. More self-aware.

I fought all the time. Often with the management. I fought about my schedule when I didn't get what I wanted. I fought with the manager I thought was an idiot, who wouldn't back up Mariana one night when she refused to serve someone without an ID. I fought with the kitchen for food coming out at the wrong time. I told myself I wrestled on behalf of the entire staff, on behalf of the guests' experience. But really, I battled for me. After fourteen months, I could no longer come to an agreement with the job. I got a new one and moved on.

VTK closed in 2009. The restaurant industry was hit hard by the recession and underpriced restaurants in downtown Chicago couldn't keep up, or maybe it was just time, the partners deciding to pivot to a different business model. The old crew gathered for a feast, sharing our favorite dishes one last time, laughing and talking shit as we always did. That's the last time I saw many of them, probably for good.

I miss my friends. Our laughter. Our arguments. The shit we talked about ourselves and our supervisors. I even miss the sensation of feeling like the stakes were high, like I had to get my life correct at twenty-four years old or I'd never figure out who I'd become, despite the notion that I was *already* becoming, no matter what I did.

Sometimes, when I think of VTK, I like to remember what

we had for a brief moment in time and imagine what could have happened had it lasted: a diverse and eclectic crew of people, who loved each other, who fought cantankerously, who stood beside one another when times got hard. Who worked hard, who pushed out food that they valued, food that could be afforded by all. People who made enough money to live in the city where they worked, to support their families, to not have to worry about bills and insurance and getting to work on time because the bus broke down or the train stopped running. People who caroused but never too mightily, except the occasional Saturday night. Who worked but weren't overworked, who made a decent wage, designed their community the way that they wanted to. Who prepared and served food that came from a real place, not a famous chef who never showed his face, who signed off on business decisions with a flick of his imperialist hand. People with no bosses. I am imagining a world that doesn't exist. Not yet. But maybe someday.

Steppenwolf

On the first morning of my new life, I sat in a cubicle and watched the summer light float through the blinds. Maybe I'd made a mistake. On my final interview, when I was offered the job, my new boss had gestured to the boxy space and said, "You'll be sitting there. I'm just across the way, so we can shout at each other. Ha!" I'd never worked in an office before and hadn't realized this work required an office. I smoothed my hands across the desktop and wondered if I'd ever feel settled.

Since I arrived in Chicago in 2004, six years prior, I'd spent my time plugging away in the city's storefront theatre community, doing what Chicago artists do best: a little bit of everything. I acted, produced storytelling festivals, production managed plays. It was exhilarating, flinging myself around the North Side of Chicago, creating a niche.

But I was approaching thirty and needed a change. I'd never done anything but wait tables, spinning between restaurants, looking for the best fit that would provide flexibility for my artistic life, quick access to cash, and a respectful work environment. Sometimes I found it; sometimes I didn't. I was burned out on serving, but I loved the ups and downs of the schedule, riding empty trains in the middle of the day, living a kind of shadow life to the normalcy on the surface.

In the summer of 2010, I found what I'd been seeking. I saw a job listing as the casting assistant at Steppenwolf Theatre Company, a Tony- and Pulitzer-lauded organization that put gritty Chicago realism on the map. I never expected to actually get the job. There were folks who knew more about casting, more about plays, that would jump to the top of the pile. But I could do something few others could, something I'd learned in my years working on the smaller Chicago arts scale: I could grind.

"Hooray, you're here!" A booming voice reverberated off the walls as my boss, Cassandra, waltzed into the office. The theatre's casting director, she carried a large file folder in her arms: stacks of that day's headshots. "We have auditions, but let's do a tour first," she said, spinning and leading me around the cubicle farm.

"These are the headshots, I'll explain how they're organized later, there's the kitchen, the coffee is *nasty*, I usually go to Starbucks for a low-fat cappuccino, no foam, extra hot. This is Nick. My *new* assistant," she introduced me to a coworker. "I'm so. Excited. He's here!" On we moved. "At some point this week, we'll sit down with the ensemble headshots, and I'll explain who everyone is, where they live, what they'll do, what they *won't* do. And then we'll talk about the School, which you will be coordinating. Did I mention that? I know it was on the job description. Wow, so much stuff. But today we're going to be with Tina. It'll be fast. Watch and listen. Trial. By. Fire."

When I chose to be an actor in high school, I discovered that all of my favorite screen actors came from this one place in Chicago. When I moved here, the aura of Steppenwolf hung everywhere; everyone I met had worked there, wanted to work there, debated each triumph or misstep. Initially, their productions didn't grab hold of me, but when I watched *The Brother/ Sister Plays*, a triptych that wove folklore, gospel, ancestry, and popular music, I realized that Steppenwolf held me, too, in its sway. A few months later, I was in the same room as Tina Landau, an ensemble member and one of the lions of our craft, the director of those plays.

At the end of the day's auditions, Cassandra and Tina discussed the two best options for the play's crucial role. They couldn't find a consensus. Both would tell the play's story.

"What do you think?" Tina asked, turning to me.

What do I think? I didn't want anyone to think I was a fraud.

"I . . . think that Joe is really sensitive and nice, but John will go deeper with the material." Tina considered my note. Cassandra nodded in satisfaction. I breathed, elated.

After work that night, I ran into my friend, William, a young director, at a bar. When I told him about the job, he slammed the table: "Everyone wanted that job!"

"Like who?" I asked.

William leaned in close. "I heard 300 people applied for it."

I took a swig of beer.

"Well, I got it," I said, with alcoholic bravado. I didn't know if I could live up to that pressure.

"You have a lot of actor friends?" he asked.

"Not really," I said. "Some."

He laughed. "You're about to."

I'd grown up attending the *Nutcracker* at the Fox Theatre in Detroit and local community plays at my high school. I was a burgeoning Shakespeare nut. I devoured the plays—*Comedy of Errors, Titus*

Nicholas Ward

Andronicus, Richard III—and obsessed over the films: Zeffirelli's *Romeo and Juliet* and *Hamlet*, Branagh's *Henry V* and *Much Ado about Nothing*, Ian McKellen's show-stopping performance as Richard III. For a rising theatre nerd, the closest option for satiating my desire was the Stratford Festival, located halfway between Detroit and Toronto. Nestled on the banks of the Avon River, it's a quaint and charming Canadian village whose entire local lifeblood revolves around the summer play festival, which consists of twelve plays in rotating repertory performed by hundreds of actors.

One summer morning in 1996, my mom and I drove two and a half hours, caught a matinee of *King Lear*, had a quick dinner, and concluded the evening with a performance of *Amadeus*. This was my entrance into contemporary theatre, and no other Shakespeare performance could match it, not then and not now.

Amadeus opens with a jolt. Whispers fill the theatre: voices gossiping at a pitch and rate just beyond our understanding, something about intrigue, something about murder. The lights rise on the old composer Antonio Salieri, now on his death bed. He looks out at us, the audience, peering into the darkened theatre. After playing a brief concerto, he appeals to us, imbues us with power, with complicity in his deeds. Suddenly, he's young again, transported to decades before, when he was the court composer for the Hapsburg Monarchy. With the audience looking on, enthralled, he spends the next three hours waging war against God by decimating His most prized earth-bound creature: Wolfgang Amadeus Mozart.

You know when someone is talking about how they met their spouse for the first time, and they'll turn to whomever they're speaking to with a twinkle in their eye and maybe a shrug, they'll say, "I just knew"? That's how I felt seeing *Amadeus*. I just knew. My entire life was laid out before me.

Steppenwolf

I drank the Steppenwolf Kool-Aid fast and full and deep. In a matter of a few months, I went from being relatively ignorant about the world of theatre to a full-on immersion: learning the language of season planning; identifying big-name actors and directors; championing small storefront artists and new play commissions; reading any plays I wanted to access; forming opinions on all of Chicago's plays; and differentiating between theatre's aesthetics; and "that didn't quite work, did it?"; making relationships with talent agents; and getting to know the forty-three member ensemble and their quirks and idiosyncrasies.

Suddenly, almost overnight, I became desirable. A fringe player in the theatre scene, I was immediately thrust into a position of power. People wanted to know me, they wanted me to know them, they wanted me to like them, and they wanted me to help them get a job. Chicago is a big city, but its art scene operates with small-town mentalities: a lot of relationship building, who you know, and getting-a-foot-in-the-door hustling. There are only about six theatres inside the city walls with a large enough budget to hire full-time staff and pay their artists living wages. We were in the top tier. Everyone wanted a piece of the Steppenwolf pie. Everyone wanted a piece of me.

Actually, most of the time it was impossible to tell what they wanted.

Once, about six months into the job, I was at a swanky downtown restaurant, having cocktails while waiting for a play reading to start. I chatted with an actress I'd auditioned that week; we'd never officially met before and so were sharing very basic getting-to-know-you information, like where we were from and what kind of theatre we'd done before. The room was loud, so we had to lean into each other a bit. When she left, my friend Jay gave me a nudge and a head nod, like *she seemed into you. Go for it.* "Nah," I said, shaking it off, "she doesn't actually like me. It's the job." Years later, that actress, now a friend, admitted to me that she was high during that interaction and nervous

Nicholas Ward

about talking to me, given my position at the theatre. It was a twisted emotional logic. I wanted the professional ascendency, but in a niche industry, that meant receiving more attention than I ever had before. That attention made me uneasy. I couldn't tell who actually liked me for me and who was trying to ingratiate themselves because they wanted a job.

In the spring of 2005, I saw the play that made me love Chicago. I'd been living in the city for a year, halfheartedly sending out my headshot and resume and trying to go on auditions. I finally got serious when I took a class at the Acting Studio and applied to intern at TPR Casting, an office right next door. This opened my world up to the Chicago I'd been looking for. Each day, I saw streams of actors roll through the casting office, each more brilliant than the next, committed with dignity to their work whether it was hawking chicken soup for a local commercial or going to the mat for a bit part in a movie. In the office, I met other interns like me, new to the business and the city, and along with the entrenched casting directors, we talked about plays and actors and what we should look for and what we should see. When Matt, the intern coordinator, and later my friend and mentor, said that a play produced in the Steppenwolf garage reinvigorated his love for Chicago theatre, I had to check it out.

Take Me Out opens with the most famous baseball player on the best team (a fictionalized version of the Yankees' Derek Jeter) coming out of the closest. The plot concerns the internal team and league-wide fallout in a sport populated by Latino and Asian immigrants and rural, white bigots. My guess is that if I saw this play now, some of the politics would feel dated. But in that space, a garage converted into a black box, the intimacy of the performances and the ease with which they handled the language rocked my world. It was everything I'd ever wanted from a play: beauty and drama and hope and heartbreak, all in one room, with actors so close that I could reach out my hands to touch them. I know now that Chicago theatre is best when it's this close, when it draws you in—not with in-your-face physical or verbal ballistics but by creating a space that we all share together.

I never cried so much at a play. The entire audience was swept up in its storm, bursting to our feet at the conclusion. The next day at the office, I couldn't stop talking about it. When the actor who played the ill-fated Davey Battle came in to audition that afternoon, I could hardly speak.

But then I noticed something strange. After he left, I asked one of my bosses, "Why was he dressed like that?"

"Oh," she said, "Anthony's a bike messenger, so he comes as is."

I fell silent, her words processing in my brain. I knew, of course, the breakdown between union and non-union actors, that it took years of effort to achieve a successful acting career. But I'd just seen him blow the roof off in an Equity production at Steppenwolf. Could he not make a life from that?

About a year into the job, I met my friend Leandra for lunch at the Whole Foods in Lincoln Park. I'd met Leandra before I started at Steppenwolf, which meant that we could talk about tacos and the new Grinderman album. But that day, she wanted to unpack the production of a Steppenwolf play, one she'd auditioned for.

"Are you going to be mad if I admit that I didn't like it?" she asked me.

"Of course not," I said.

"It was just . . ." she said, sighing. "No one was in their body, No one seemed like their real selves. It was slow."

As a Neo-Futurist, Leandra was consumed with speed and a lack of presentation.

"I think you don't like the Steppenwolf aesthetic," I said. "That's okay."

I stood up to leave.

"Where are you going?" Leandra asked.

"I gotta go back to work."

"No," she said with a frown, "you don't get a full hour?"

"I do," I said, "but we have an all-staff at two and I gotta debrief from the summer and set my interns up with projects and I don't want to stay late, cuz I'm seeing four plays this week."

Leandra put a hand out to me. "You don't have to do this."

"What do you mean?" I asked.

"If this isn't the job you want, you don't have to work it."

"Of course I do," I said. "I mean, I beat out hundreds of people to get it. Earlier this year, I got to call twenty-eight students and tell them they got into the School at Steppenwolf. I got to make their dreams come true."

Later that day, at the all-staff meeting in the downstairs theatre, Martha Lavey, the artistic director, stood poised behind a podium, glasses perched on her nose. "As you all know," she said, "we have completed one of the most successful seasons in the company's history, an artistic triumph that featured a masterful new understanding of *Who's Afraid of Virginia Woolf?* We've just come from a meeting with our New York producers, and I'm pleased to announce that we're orchestrating a Broadway transfer."

The staff sat in silence. Then the whole room burst into applause.

On the way back to the office, I caught up with Cassandra.

"I'm doing the understudy casting on this in New York," she said, as we stopped traffic on Halsted walking back across the street. "If you have time today, can you call all of the talent agents for the role of Honey and ask them for their measurements?"

"Whose measurements?" I asked.

"The actresses'," she said. "She's called a 'little mousy thing' in the script and we need to make sure that everyone who comes in fits that description."

It dawned on me what I was being asked to do. "Oh," I said.

From my cubicle, headshots laid out in front of me, thank

you cards from actors taped to the felt wall behind me, I took an anxious breath. "Hi, this is Nick calling from Steppenwolf Theatre Company in Chicago. Will the actresses you submitted for the role of Honey please send me their hip, waist, and bust measurements?" I slammed the phone down as fast as I could, my face white with shame, hoping a coworker couldn't hear me as they zoomed past. But I didn't stop. I found an empty conference room, plugged in a phone, and made those calls where no one could listen.

My first Steppenwolf paycheck almost caused me to choke on my dinner. I knew that I'd be taking a pay cut to work there, that the $26,000 yearly salary plus benefits and a 401k was the sacrifice I'd have to make for working in an arts organization. I just didn't realize, after taxes and health care and retirement, what that money meant on a week-by-week basis. For the first year, I made exactly $738 on a two-week, eighty-hour pay period, which was roughly what I could make working four or five nights at a restaurant.

Coming from some financial privilege allowed me to accept the job in the first place. My parents were both teachers at a time when teachers' salaries, benefits packages, pensions, and social security were extremely well-funded. They made a really good living. My father navigated the minefield of financial investments shrewdly and safely, with a sizable rainy day fund if anything calamitous should happen. If I faltered financially, my parents could send grocery money, help with a month's rent, or buy me a new coat for winter. From the Roscoe Village neighborhood where I lived, I rode my bike or took the train to work. With close proximity to good, safe public transit, I didn't need to purchase a car and make expensive payments. My class status, the net below me I knew I could fall into, afforded me the opportunity to work a job whose median weekly earnings were consistent with minimum wage employment.

Nicholas Ward

I knew this was the trade-off of having a job in the arts, but here's another thing I know now: in the nonprofit world, if it seems like you enjoy doing something, there is an assumption that you will want to do it for free. I liked seeing plays. One of the great perks of my job was the access to theatre tickets pretty much whenever I wanted them, but it was my job to see plays, to watch and assess actors. It was work I was never paid for. If I spent five hours watching plays a week (sometimes more, sometimes less), I didn't get overtime for that, and I didn't get an opportunity to take five hours off my forty-hour-a-week office schedule somewhere else. When I checked my email on nights and weekends, I rarely got thanked verbally and never financially for spending my non-work time working. On the flip side, there were many moments over those three years when I had absolutely no work to accomplish but still had to sit at my desk, fucking around on social media.

My second week on staff, after I'd been trained and begun to settle in, I noticed that no one in the office talked. Restaurants are constant streams of chatter: the guests laughing or arguing or asking questions, the staff constantly naming their movements —"Behind you / On your left / Can I get that on the fly? / I gotta pee, watch my section"—such that no one gets cut or bumped into or breaks glassware. Chefs call out orders to the cooks who respond with affirmations, expos ask for hands to run food, servers talk shit about their guests or other servers. I didn't realize how much I would miss that noise. I loved the energy of it, the whirling parts all working together towards a common goal. Making plays and events was like that too—all the running around, calling people, dashing off emails, painting sets, hauling lumber, showing up every day with your fellow actors. It felt like good, solid, honest work.

Steppenwolf was a revelation. I'd wanted a life in theatre because I didn't think I could live an office-based, nine-to-five life, but that's exactly what I'd fallen into. If somebody needed something, they'd email you, even if you sat right next to them. No one ever played music publicly. People just sat at their desks and plunked away. If they needed to meet, they reserved rooms. It was strange.

One winter morning, I arrived at work before the sun came up. Around 8:30, I wiped a few-days-old coffee stain from my desk and settled into my morning emails. My stomach went south. One of the actors coming in for callbacks that morning hadn't gotten their sides when I sent them out the night before. This was bad. Actors need time to prepare, and we had only given them one night. Now this guy hadn't gotten them until the morning. I double-checked the emails that I'd sent to his agent, a recently retired icon of Chicago theatre and film who now worked part-time from home. The only reason we worked with her anymore was because she was Cassandra's good friend. The callback sides were attached to the emails I sent to her and all the other talent agents. No one else had any problems. It was an honest mistake.

Cassandra didn't see it that way. The moment she walked in the office, she stuck her head over my cubicle.

"You fucked up. You can never do that ever again. That is unacceptable behavior."

I tried to talk, but she walked away.

A friend in a nearby cubicle sent me an email. "You okay?" she asked.

I wasn't.

In restaurants, the chefs are particularly volatile creatures. But if, as a server, you get yelled at by the chef, you say "fuck it," walk out of the kitchen and pour as much into your tables as possible. Chefs don't directly control your access to income. There are plenty of ways to funnel a browbeating into something useful, and there are a plethora of restaurants in Chicago; if you bounce around long enough, you will eventually find people who will treat you with care and respect.

Nicholas Ward

At Steppenwolf, I worked for someone who happened to be one of the five most important and influential people in a niche field with little opportunity for other forms of employment. I'd beaten out 300 people for my job. Those other people were not making their living in theatre. There were plenty of other incidents not worth mentioning, but I remember hitting my breaking point one day after she told me that "I needed to step up," that my work performance was poor. I was putting in more than 40 hours in the office, staying at least an hour late every day, checking emails on nights and weekends, seeing a minimum of two plays each week, and putting in work as a company member with not one but two other theatre companies. I made roughly $14 an hour before taxes, without accounting for the extra work. I didn't know how much I had to give. But rather than advocating for myself, rather than suggesting that I might work better if we restructured my time there, I took it. After all, I'd made it to the top! I'd beaten out 300 people! My path towards a viable, salaried career in theatre, something that so many other people sought, was laid out for me. This is true about theatre, too: it creates a vacuum that elevates those deemed exceptional and then uses the terms of their success against them.

I wasn't the only one. The old model of a rigorous nine-to-five work life and the new technology that made constant work possible overlapped in unhealthy and dangerous ways. The stress in that office was palpable. I saw senior-level management get a dressing down from the top brass, good people walk out the door because they no longer could justify taking it, junior-level staff burst into tears. I watched as people's ideas were shot down, as taste was adjudicated by those at the top. And over three years, I stood by as nonwhite voices were simultaneously disregarded and exceptionalized.

Steppenwolf, and many theatres of their size, talked a great game about inclusion and opportunity. But when it comes down to it, these organizations remain hierarchical institutions that reinforce white supremacy. An old-moneyed (often white) patron class purchase expensive season subscriptions at $60 per play. This, along with an impressive, ongoing fundraising and development campaign, allows Steppenwolf to build a $14 million per year budget. The plays produced push the boundaries of American theatre, but they can only go so far. Steppenwolf can't afford to alienate their base. Instead, they use their prestige to sell tickets. If a patron gets to see a star like Jimmy Smits, up close and personal in a play, they might more easily ingest a foul-mouthed production about marital infidelity and New Yorkers who talk a lot of motherfucking shit. Art and commerce make poor bedfellows, but this avenue is often the only route towards getting an audience member to care about a challenging play. It's a delicate dance, and I have both sympathy for those who try to tap it out and derision that it needs to exist at all. What I found in my time at Steppenwolf, seeing plays both at home and around the city, is that the large theatres in Chicago can never really push an audience too hard. It's not that gritty Chicago realism can't exist on the big stage or that theatres that have grown into large institutions have abandoned that aesthetic. It's that gritty Chicago realism is a house of cards ill-equipped for grappling with the substantive demands of a changing world quite like the plurality of voices I thought I'd find on Steppenwolf stages.

"None of the Black ensemble members want to play slaves," my boss told me in my first week on the job. No shit, I thought. The available roles for nonwhite artists are both scant and limiting. From 2010 to 2013, in the fifteen main-stage productions, nine of them featured at least one person of color. Of those nine plays, seven of them were written by white people: one was about the Civil War; four featured two or less nonwhite actors. The four plays that featured a larger number of nonwhite actors were directed by two woman directors who actively believed in decentering whiteness onstage. Only one production featured more than two

Nicholas Ward

races onstage at the same time, and it was Chekhov's *Three Sisters*, a play written over one hundred years ago. In other words, there were very specific boxes to check, and only those boxes were open to people of color. Of the fifteen plays, fourteen were directed by white people, and thirteen were written by white people.

In recent years, new artistic leadership and heightened national conversations about the ways our stages look, and which stories they tell, has led Steppenwolf to restructure who writes, directs, and stars in their plays. The ensemble has changed dramatically, from an older white collection of artists to a younger generation of Black and Latinx artists far more representative of Chicago than ever before. The plays produced are bold in new ways, exploring new themes as new voices push away from the hegemony of old. I see it as an outsider now. My connections to the storied institution are mostly severed. I don't know what goes on behind closed doors, but the theatre is still a massive arts institution with an annual budget in the tens of millions (less than most NBA starters, more than most arts organizations). I have to imagine the systemic issues still remain; they can't be waved away that easily. Even from afar, the financials rankle. In 2019, Steppenwolf broke ground on a $73 million expansion: a lavish new theatre space and education wing. If they could raise that much money, I thought, I wondered why they paid their workers a barely livable wage. When the coronavirus pandemic forced all stages to close for the unforeseeable future, Steppenwolf made dramatic cuts to its staff. Longtime staff members, people who had served venerably for decades, were let go. I know that capital projects don't work like this, but a multi-million-dollar building sitting empty while people lose their livelihoods seems like a statement of values louder than any play programmed on their stages.

There are moments I will never forget: watching Tracy Letts and Amy Morton tear up the rehearsal room before tearing up

Broadway in *Who's Afraid of Virginia Woolf?* en route to earning three Tony Awards; sitting in on a Shakespearean acting class with one of the world's foremost Shakespearean acting teachers and members of the Steppenwolf ensemble—the finest actors in Chicago; shepherding a group of doe-eyed acting students through a series of tumultuous summers, watching them blossom with love for each other and the process.

Some mornings, when I didn't have work at my desk, or even before a long day, I'd walk into the balcony of the rehearsal room, Yondorf Hall. Once a ballroom back in the era of manicured social dances, the grand, high-ceilinged room was as close to a place of worship as anywhere on site. To observe Yondorf was to note the rituals of our shared collaborations. There we surrounded the artists in a circle on the first rehearsal day, introducing ourselves to a new group. Tape marked the floors, simulating the unbuilt set, the world created by those ephemeral bodies and minds, disappearing the moment it begun. When I was feeling generous, I'd marvel at how close I stood to artistic greatness. It was fool's gold. Once I realized I'd never be allowed to cross the threshold, that I only existed to help make the art, not actively participate, I began to want what I couldn't have. I wasn't ungrateful; it was just that I needed to prioritize the work I truly believed in.

On my last day, I went shopping in Wicker Park, buying myself a fancy Chrome bag as a going-away present. When I returned, the air conditioning had kicked, and there was a sign on the door announcing the office had closed early.

"Hello?" I said, new bag slung over my shoulder while I poked around the empty desks. No one was there. If I'd expected a hero's sendoff, I wasn't going to get it. I didn't deserve it anyway. The job had been a plateau, not a bridge. And not the answer to the question of my life.

By the time I finished cleaning out my desk, it was just as I'd

Nicholas Ward

found it three years prior. On Monday, my replacement would begin. I'd trained her without being honest about the job. She'd find out soon enough.

Career Opportunities

We'd been told not to talk, that all questions would be answered at the end. Nobody knew what to expect.

Around nine thirty, all of us—the servers, bartenders, and food runners—all congregated in the semi-secluded, three-season patio, bantering playfully, taking bets on who'd get yelled at first and how late we'd be kept. The mood had been jovial that Thursday night. The guests were friendly and their tips were good. The front of house staff was happy to close an hour early to try the lunch menu being unveiled the following day.

I'd been working at the "French-ish" bistro on the North Side of Ann Arbor, Michigan for a few months. At that point in my life, I was a lot closer to the end of my twenty-year serving career than the beginning, though I didn't know it at the time. I thought the food at the bistro was boring and overpriced, the floor overstaffed, and the design choices kitschy and poorly conceived. But I'd found my niche as an experienced server committed to providing excellent guest experiences without taking myself too seriously. I got along well with the staff and even looked forward to working with certain people. Some nights, I actually liked the job.

A few minutes past ten, we were joined by the managers, chefs, and the owner, Aaron. He launched into one of his long-winded speeches, about how opening for lunch would be a unique opportunity to bring our brand to a new dining sector in this part of town.

As the successful restaurateur of Mexican and Italian concepts in Ann Arbor's quaint downtown area, closer to campus, and a former Chicago ad executive, Aaron loved to hear himself talk. Deep into the bottle of vodka he allegedly finished each night (along with rumors of coke and pills), he couldn't be stopped. After each of the first two dishes, he asked our opinions, eliciting questions about the flavors and preparation techniques. Pretty soon, people spoke over each other, the quiet tasting transforming into a more relaxed atmosphere.

"How many ounces is this?" Stevie, one of the bartenders, inquired about a lamb sausage.

"Four," I said, referencing our tasting sheet.

He asked the same question of the next dish, a bit of curried chicken salad.

Aaron, foot out the door on his way back to the kitchen, spun around.

"We don't ask that here," he said, tersely.

I jumped in. "Yeah, but those of us who haven't worked for the company for years don't know that." I'd been there four months while some coworkers had been employed there since the opening of the first restaurant.

"We don't ask that question," Aaron said, turning to me. "We don't say that to our guests."

"But Stevie's not gonna say that to the guests. He's just curious."

Aaron's voice rose. "I said it on the last fucking dish."

"I'm sorry. I misheard you."

Aaron narrowed his eyes. I realized everyone had stopped talking. "You misheard me?"

I shrugged. "I guess I didn't hear."

He jutted his face forward.

"Listen."

He left, slamming the doors behind him. I threw my hoodie over my head, buried my face down. No one spoke. A few people risked furtive glances in my direction. Otherwise, they didn't meet my eyes.

A moment later, Aaron was back.

"Nick, can I see you outside?" His round face beckoned from the doorway, cheeks red. I stood up, stuffing my hands into the pockets of my hooded sweatshirt. I followed him to the main dining room.

Prior to that moment, Aaron and I had gotten along well. He clapped me on the back whenever he saw me, his large hands thundering against my shoulders. He was half a foot taller than me and at least seventy-five pounds heavier, a bull of a man with a large gut and a barrel chest. His reputation for losing his cool preceded him, but I thought he trusted my instincts and opinions. On New Year's Eve, just a few weeks before, we drank bubbly after hours while he asked my thoughts on putting a new seafood tower on the menu. I figured I was safe.

Aaron pivoted and faced me down. "Pack your shit and go."

I opened my mouth to protest, to indicate that I had meant no disrespect. I didn't get a word out. Aaron unleashed a string of expletives, an explosion of vitriol. It would've been impressive if it wasn't directed at me, about how I'm an asshole and arrogant and insubordinate and he doesn't want me talking to "his" guests. He was so close to me, consuming my physical space. If I tried to walk away, I worried he would grab me and fling me like a rag doll.

Nicholas Ward

"Back in there, that's how assholes talk," Aaron continued, "you are an asshole and I don't have assholes working for me. So pack your shit and go."

He huffed and panted, physically exhausted. I looked at him and shrugged.

"Okay."

I had met people like Aaron throughout my entire career working in restaurants, which began in 1998.

In high school, the manager at the family diner, who was only a few years older than me, used to bark at servers who stood around during their shift: "If you've got time to lean, you've got time to clean!"

In my college restaurant job, the sous chef, who'd worked lines everywhere between Arizona and Ohio, once tossed a kitchen knife in the direction of a twenty-year-old server, who held back tears for the rest of the night. When my friend and I informed the owner, he dismissed us, muttering, "Don't judge a man until you've walked in his shoes."

The first chef I worked for in Chicago would fly into fits of apoplectic fury over the mildest infractions, like ringing in an order incorrectly. My favorite threat of his: "If you don't get your shit together, I'll take that book away right now," as though without one's notes, one is no longer a server. I saw him fire people on the spot. I also worked for the man twice and watched him show restraint with people undergoing a personal rough patch.

When scrolling back through the Rolodex of my serving life, if I wonder about who the asshole in the restaurant was, I know it was me. Brash and arrogant, I was unapologetic in what I wanted, which was often more tables to wait on and more money in my pocket. When I bartended for a brief spell in college, I demanded that the serving staff bring me what I needed when I asked for it. When a slightly younger server asked me to be a little bit nicer, I snapped at her: "Bring me what I want, when I want it." When I went back to waiting tables, I got into it with bartenders who behaved in the same way. I could barely see that my status allowed me to act that way. Subconsciously, maybe I knew that unless I really crossed the line into immoral, unethical, or illegal behavior, I'd never be disciplined. At one of my early Chicago stops, I derided the lead partner, who'd show up every few days to lecture us on etiquette, serving techniques, and lead condescending motivational speeches. All my coworkers liked him. When I asked them why they couldn't see his obvious arrogance, one of them said, "You don't like him because you're basically the same person." I suspect that's why Aaron and I initially got along and also why I was fired so quickly. He didn't appreciate any threats to his power, and I didn't have any actual power myself. As a server, and never a manager or an owner, my arrogance could only take me so far.

Every time I stepped into a restaurant, I knew the risks. I also had it easy. Half of the lowest-paying jobs in the US are in food service. Line cooks and dishwashers make minimum wage for long hours of backbreaking work. Bussers and food runners receive less but get tipped out from the servers and bartenders. Even the best support staff almost always has to work two jobs. Women in the industry face the highest rates of discrimination of any field in the country. As a cisgender, white man with a college degree and a career spent in medium-to-high-end restaurants, I seemed to fall just beneath the executive chefs, owners, and mixologists in the proverbial food chain.

Even for me, that work was precarious. Few establishments offer benefits. Those that do provide paid time off do so at the sub-tipped minimum wage ($2.13 on the Federal level). Sick days are nonexistent. Towards the beginning of winter, a manager would say, "Okay everyone, it's moving into cold and flu season. Get your shots. Drink lots of tea. Wash your hands. And if you do get sick, take NyQuil."

Nicholas Ward

I worry about the toll that life exacted on my psyche. I wonder what it meant to jump around so often, unsatisfied, restless, working wildly different hours from gig to gig, making good money to travel or take time off but never plunging anything meaningful into savings. I knew people who stayed at the same restaurant for years, who found their stability. That wasn't me. In twenty years, I worked in twenty different restaurants, some for only a few weeks at a time. I suspected I might be in love with the squall, the noise and chaos, the temperament my life in restaurants created. Towards the end, I worried about my body. I once asked two former coworkers—all of us in our mid- to late thirties—how people get old in the business. They both looked at me with helpless, faraway eyes. "I don't know," they said. Servers stand on their feet for eight to twelve hours at a clip. Eventually, bodies will break down. What happens after that?

In truth, that restaurant group in Ann Arbor offered some fine perks: health, dental, and vision benefits at a good rate, stable income. Many of my coworkers were with them for five years plus. It baffled me. Servers, bartenders, bussers, and cooks had to wear company T-shirts specific to each restaurant, like the corporate job lampooned in the movie *Waiting*. An employee handbook described a list of ten platitudes we were expected to memorize, like "Attitude of gratitude," and insisted that if we had problems with the management or the owner, we should feel empowered to take it up with the HR representative, who just happened to be Aaron's wife. On paper, that creates a robust work environment. But since one person was the head bull in all the china shops, the whole enterprise was smoke and mirrors.

I've had managers stick up for their staff. When my friend got sent home from my first job in Chicago, it was the managers that calmed down the chef, sending my friend away with a message of reassurance. When that same friend became my manager later on, he endured a litany of abuse that he never passed on to the staff. Even later, at our third restaurant together, my friend insisted that a sous chef apologize to me, technically the subordinate, for yelling at me in the middle of a shift.

I could have used my friend that January night. If I expected my manager, Bobbie, to defend me to her boss, I received the answer in an email later that evening. "I think you made a bad decision. You were arguing with the owner in front of the staff. It wasn't worth trying to defend Stevie." No acknowledgement of Aaron's behavior or his presumed intoxication or his language. In the moral relativism of restaurant culture, what I did was wrong, but I detest the implication that sticking up for a coworker wasn't worth it.

Later that Thursday night, after the shock had worn off, I sat on my couch with a bottle of whiskey. It was the night before the inauguration of Trump. I reflected sentimentally—and uncritically—on Obama, reading the articles and tweets and posts, desperate for him to stay and terrified of what was to come. In that haze, I convinced myself I behaved righteously. That I stood up to a tyrant. That I defended my fellow man. That in times like these, we were going to need more people like me.

The next night, I met up with Jon, a now former coworker. Over beers, we bitched about Aaron and the culture of the place, how he was free to operate with unchecked aggression.

"That kinda happened to me," Jon said.

"Huh?" I asked.

"With Aaron. Right when the restaurant opened, in the summer, before you worked there. I'd been gettin' the shit section every night, those happy hour high-tops where people spend, like, twenty bucks and stay there all night. And everybody else had outside tables and large parties and was rolling in it; it's summer, everyone's happy, and I'm like, 'Maybe somethin' is wrong with me.' Ya know, I kinda felt like the odd man out. I've never worked for the company; I don't know anybody. So I ask Bobbie one day before the shift. We're sitting in the office, and

Nicholas Ward

I say, 'Look. I'm a good server. I have a few decades of experience. I know a lot about wine and food. Is there a reason that you're keeping me on the leash?' And Aaron, I don't know how he heard me, but he comes flying back into the office, and he just lays into me. Same as you. 'You're an asshole. You're ungrateful. Blah blah blah.' And, at some point during his tirade, I just stand up and I don't say anything and I look him right in the eyes."

Jon, it should be mentioned, is six feet, five inches tall. Twenty-five years before, he played in the toughest college basketball program in the country. He was drafted to play professional baseball. He doesn't take shit from anybody and he doesn't have to.

"What happened?" I asked.

He smiled. "He shut right the fuck up. Hasn't really talked to me since."

I spent Thursday night thinking I'd rather it be me than Stevie, the bartender who started this mess. His wife had just given birth to their first child. My partner and I lived simply, in a two-bedroom with our cat. We were just passing through here. Better me than him.

That's not what happened. After I left, according to Jon, the entire room went dead silent. A bomb could have gone off and no one would've batted an eyelash. They tasted the food in silence. Then, Aaron swung through again and pulled Stevie out and gave him the same vicious dressing down. And Stevie walked out too.

It's a fickle profession. Guests control the access to income; owners and managers control the access to guests. Many servers and bartenders live night to night, paycheck to paycheck. It can all fall apart at any moment, which is why it's so moving when communities band together. After a fire at Chicago's Lost Lake forced the popular tiki bar to close for a few weeks in 2016, bars around the city held Lost Lake pop-ups. Servers and bartenders sacrificed a night of income to allow their competitors to make money while they waited for their joint to reopen. Detroit's Takoi went up in flames too, and a Kickstarter began immediately to help the restaurant get back on its feet and find employees jobs while they lingered in uncertainty.

Initially, I was frustrated that not one person said anything in my or Stevie's defense when we were kicked aside. How could they just sit there with their heads down? But I was proved wrong. The next day, Dionne hipped me to a job opening at another restaurant, and Jon told his friend, Melinda, who knew the manager Mary well enough to give me a recommendation. The bartender there, Cecilia, was best friends with Dionne's sister, and she helped me feel welcome from day one. It was a good fit: chef-driven, a small, tight-knit staff, an opportunity to be myself. But like all the others, it didn't last very long.

Johnny's Grill

The winter before I left Chicago for my sojourn in Ann Arbor, I took a job waiting tables at Johnny's Grill in Logan Square. I'd just returned from a writing residency, and my partner, Nima, had been accepted at the grad school of her choice. We'd be moving at the end of summer. I needed money. Fast.

At the interview, the restaurant was in disarray. They'd closed for a few days of remodeling to open a mezcal bar next door; the cooler was shoved into the middle of the diner, and plastic tarps covered the other surfaces. This wasn't the Johnny's I remembered from my first years living in the city, but the stools and Formica countertops all looked the same.

Afterwards, I met my friend Molly for coffee at Reno across the square. Reno had once been Abril, a Mexican restaurant where I dined my first night in Chicago. Reno looked out onto the Illinois Centennial Monument, a tall column with an eagle affixed to the top, that connected Logan and Kedzie boulevards, and thus formed the Square. From the long bank of windows, I could see the big, red Norwegian church and the L station recently beatified with a community garden and a neighborhood-approved wall of street art.

"You interviewed at Johnny's?" Molly asked. "You know I work for that company?"

"No idea," I said. We sat at a long wooden community table while the Reno staff transitioned from lunch to dinner service.

"They took over the space last year," she said. "Sarah, the chef, is amazing, just so brilliant. I'll put in a good word for you." Molly worked as the editor for the restaurant group's culture website.

"Thank you," I said. "Please don't tell them I'm moving."

"Your secret is safe with me," she said. "Plus, this way we'll get to hang before you go."

Molly and I have been friends for over a decade. She and her husband lived on Richmond Ave near Palmer Square in a two-flat that he'd bought with a friend. I'd moved into my girlfriend's apartment in Pilsen the previous summer.

"I'm not that excited to come up here every day," I said. "It's so different from even a year ago."

Molly made a loud guffaw. "Ugh, I know. I was drunk with Malachy last night after dinner, yelling loudly about it on our walk home. 'These damn interlopers!' I said."

"Interlopers?"

"Interlopers!" She laughed. "Everything has changed so quickly from what it used to be, and it makes me so sad."

The truth is that Molly and I were interlopers, too. Though her family's roots are in old-school Irish Chicago and her husband was born and raised in Edgewater, Molly is from outside Minneapolis. After college, I arrived to Logan Square with no sense of purpose beyond my own forward-moving trajectory. I fell hard for my first neighborhood in Chicago. I loved the way the boulevard exploded from under the Kennedy's viaduct, the stately greystones that lined the wide street, the live music on Saturdays at the Winds Cafe, the smell of fried plantains wafting across the bar, the cheap rundown movie theatre on Milwaukee Avenue, where five bucks bought a ticket and a bag of popcorn, and of course, Johnny's Grill: the quintessential greasy spoon, perfect for sopping up last night's booze. Open since 1971, Johnny's was truly a gem. When the Art Institute of Chicago was promoting their Edward Hopper exhibit, they chose Johnny's as the iconic Chicago locale for a remix of Hopper's *Nighthawks*. Even though the diner was hopping during a weekend morning, the brooding, late-night loneliness depicted there felt prophetic.

I'm romanticizing the time I spent in Logan Square out of proportion. My memory is filtered through the knowledge of what happened to the neighborhood. Most of the time I lived in Logan Square, I spent my free time elsewhere, in River North where I worked, or Wicker Park, the hipster playground, or Southport Corridor, where I auditioned for plays. Now, that time far in my rearview mirror, I'm free to wax nostalgic about "the way it used to be," whether or not I supported that way of life when I lived there. After just two years in Logan Square, I moved to Roscoe Village.

In 2013, a full seven years after I left Logan Square, I moved back. Everything had changed. According to Census data, in the fourteen years between 2000 and 2014, the Latino population in Logan had decreased by 35 percent, while the white population had increased by 47 percent. The Winds Cafe, once owned by Black Caribbean residents, had transformed into Longman & Eagle, a Michelin-star pig and whiskey joint run by a concept development studio called Land & Sea Dept. The Logan Theatre was remodeled into a bar with craft beer installed in an adjacent room. A real estate developer named M. Fishman was buying up properties and leveraging old tenants to move at an alarming rate. An abandoned rail line was in the process of being turned into a city park and a wide bike path connecting the east to the west. Not all the changes were being made at the hands of mustache-twirling developers and the new middle-class residents who wanted to remake the neighborhood in their image. Logan Square Preservation is a nonprofit organization that has existed since at least the mid-1980s. One of their first initiatives, one they still boast as a success on their website, was to close a walkway tunnel that connected two streets under the Kennedy Expressway. That closing something is the opposite of preservation is an irony apparently lost on them. The justification pointed to "gang activity," a racist canard that refuses to account for any underlying systemic conditions and, as a straw man, can't be argued against. Their main efforts have been to preserve the history and beauty of the neighborhood but maintaining historic properties requires the kind of money that most working-class families don't have and often makes it impossible for new affordable housing to be built anywhere near all that history. I'm sure that Logan Square Preservation loves the neighborhood as much as anyone else. However, since they've been able to muster political power for their initiatives, that indicates (without ever actually saying it out loud) who they believe the neighborhood is really for. Additionally, they would dine at Johnny's often and were the worst kind of regulars, those who believe the restaurant exists to serve them and them alone. Since they've been in the neighborhood so long, my guess is that they would balk at being labeled gentrifiers, but the Logan Square they built—or helped preserve —went a long way towards making that area an attractive destination for artists priced out of Wicker Park, college graduates new to the city, and restaurateurs looking for their next venture. The developers just followed all that new money.

Shortly before I moved back to the neighborhood, I had a conversation with someone at a party who wanted to know why I lived in Roscoe Village, the neighborhood catty-corner to

Nicholas Ward

Logan in the northeast, where I'd spent most of the interim years. We were congregated on the cement slab in the back of an apartment building in Logan.

"I like it in Roscoe," I told her. "It's well-positioned for how I move through the city; it's pretty, and there's a good bar at the end of my street."

"It's so boring," she said. "It's all babies and dogs everywhere."

I wanted to ask what she thought Logan Square was becoming. I wanted to ask what she thought Logan Square used to be, before its gentrification began. But, I knew I couldn't find an inroad; she was invested in Logan Square as the only neighborhood that mattered in Chicago, and there was no talking her out of it, but I wondered if she'd feel the same about the neighborhood in ten years.

My second era in Logan was marked by falling out of love with Dina and then back in love with Nima. In the summer of 2013, I moved into one of those beautiful greystones along Logan Boulevard. Dina and I took over a second-floor unit, still affordable on our arts admin salaries, where we strung lights across the back deck and hosted elaborate parties that lasted well into the night. That winter, after we broke up, I moved into a bungalow on a side street with a dog and two housemates who would save my emotional life. Our landlord, a Polish lawyer originally from Pilsen, lived upstairs with his two cats. He never renovated the downstairs flat, so he never raised the rent. I fell in love with Nima, who lived in Pilsen. For almost a year, I was back and forth between Logan Square, the West Loop (where I worked), and Pilsen, stopping home to drink cheap beers from cold mugs at Helen's Two-Way Lounge with my roommate, Erika, or watch my cat and her dog run around our apartment together.

Before, there were a handful of inexpensive food options, places like Café con Leche, El Cid, Puebla—Mexican-run restaurants that had been in the neighborhood for years. On my return, a host of new spots popped up: L'Patron Tacos, founded by alums of Rick Bayless's kitchens; Cellar Door Provisions, which sold the finest bread in the neighborhood; Bang Bang Pie, a pie stand first run from the owner's home, now expanded into an actual space. There were a bevy of craft cocktail bars (Billy Sunday, Scofflaw, Lost Lake) where once there had only been The Whistler. There were breweries and fine-dining restaurants and coffee roasters and it all just seemed like too much for me. Too much commerce; too much developmental one-upsmanship. I scoffed when others referred to Logan Square as a hot neighborhood on the rise. I knew, at least a little bit, what it had looked like before. I wasn't thrilled by what it had become, but I didn't want to fully consider how people like me had made it that way. Now I understand that, by my presence alone, I represented a shift in not only how the neighborhood looked but in how it functioned. I may not personally have wanted to remake Logan Square in whatever image I held in mind of a hip, urbane community, and clearly, I hold some antagonism for the preservationists. But I was a member of the class who had no personal history there, no roots or connections. That made it easy for me to flock to the new bars and restaurants. Only my affection for The Winds prevented me from loving Longman like everybody else did. But when I was a five-minute walk from L'Patron and CDP, I went there all the time. Even my celebration of The Whistler being a pre-gentrification bar is an indicator, as that spot opened after I moved to Chicago and after I'd left the neighborhood for the first time. I just liked it better than the others. I remember one St. Patrick's Day Saturday—where Chicago's white residents pour out of every stupid sports bar in Wrigleyville and Lincoln Park—I biked past a bar on California Avenue on my way to work where the same thing was happening. "Logan Square has jumped the shark," I posted on Facebook. I may have wanted to distance myself, but I know I contributed just as much as anybody else.

Nicholas Ward

Somewhere in that period, Johnny's Grill closed. Nicholas Kalliantsis, the longtime proprietor, didn't want to leave, he said, but the owner of the building decided not to renew his lease. My social media pages were awash in mourning, from both new Logan Square residents and those who had grown up in the neighborhood. For the old-timers, it represented one of the last stalwarts of the old way of life. For the newcomers, it represented the exact same thing but refracted through a different mechanism. Johnny's was unique in that way, a tether between the eras. Whether it wanted to be or not, the restaurant was a buffer against the neighborhood's transformation into the dreaded middlebrow consumerism on display in Wicker Park and Bucktown, full of upscale retail stores and chain conveniences. Gentrification was already on the move northwest along the CTA Blue Line that connected these neighborhoods. Johnny's demise, then, was a symbol; it threatened to break the neighborhood open, transforming Logan Square for eternity.

Into the Johnny's void stepped a restaurant/real estate group, who won a contested bidding war for the rights to the space on the corner of the Square, the hottest real estate property in Chicago. The old Johnny's became the new Johnny's.

At first, I couldn't help but giggle, watching the hipster servers stand behind guests sitting at the diner's counter. They couldn't serve from the counter itself, as that was where the line was. The approach was all polished and professional. It seemed like they were trying too hard to graft a hospitality-based experience onto a space meant for slinging burgers. I entered into Johnny's with some complicated feelings about working there, about being one of the many faces of the new Logan Square. But I didn't have an opportunity to reflect on it much at the time. I was there with a singular purpose: fast cash.

On my first morning, I followed one of the lead servers during a busy brunch while she explained to me the menu, flow, layout, etc. I'd briefly met the head chef, Sarah, a rising star in the food world, an award-winning pastry chef who'd organized the menu around classic diner fare crafted with care, alongside some favorites from her native country of Ireland. Over eighteen years in the industry, I'd never worked for a woman chef before. I'd never worked in a restaurant where the kitchen was majority women. In an industry that did the same thing over and over again, it was refreshing to find a new environment.

At one point during that first service, a Saturday brunch, Chef Sarah asked me to get some potatoes from the downstairs prep area. "Go get 'em, tiger," she said, whacking me on the ass with her chef's towel. I stopped. I thought briefly about saying something like, "hey, that's not really appropriate." I thought about how it was my first day and I needed money. I got Sarah the potatoes.

When I came back up, Jessica, my trainer, pulled me aside. "I just want to tell you that I saw what happened and that's not okay and we will deal with it," she said. Later, after the rush, the GM, Jessie, came over. "Hey, I heard about a little incident that happened with Chef Sarah," she told me. "I want you to know that I've spoken with her about it and that it will not happen again. We want to make sure that you feel safe here."

"Thank you," I said, "that means a lot to me."

I don't wish to explain away Sarah's behavior. We worked together later on and occasionally joked about that moment. "Hey, remember when I smacked your ass on the first day you worked for me?" she'd say. "Yeah, that was really inappropriate," I'd respond. I wonder how much sexual harassment she had had to endure coming up from male cooks? How many times did a head chef speak or act inappropriately to a subordinate and not have a general manager rein in his power? It was, in fact, the way that the leadership of Johnny's handled that situation that endeared me to them. So many other restaurants would have let that slide.

From the moment Johnny's re-opened, there was attention.

Nicholas Ward

Restaurant critics and media outlets wrote about it in ways they never had about the previous iteration. That attention intensified when the Mezcaleria Las Flores, the city's first mezcal-focused cocktail bar, opened next door; it was a colorful space with hanging flowerpots and turquoise walls complete with a painted map of Mexico. At the same time, around when I began working there in February of 2016, Sarah's burger started receiving outsized praise. Two thin patties finished with sea salt, gooey melted cheese, and mustard aioli, the *Chicago Tribune* compared it favorably against Au Cheval's burger, the most famous sandwich in the nation. *Chicago Magazine, Chicago Reader, Eater Chicago*, all hyped the burger. Steve Dolinsky, the local NBC host of *Hungry Hound*, dropped by with a camera crew and that brought out the suburban crowd—people driving in from an hour away to have a $9 burger at our neighborhood diner. It was absurd.

Despite my hesitations about the new Johnny's, it was also maybe the best job I have ever had. Perhaps it was because I knew that I was leaving, that there was an end date, that made it easier to wake up early on the weekends and slog through a grueling brunch shift. But maybe, if I'm being really honest with myself, it's because I believed in something about the place. This Johnny's represented a changing neighborhood; it couldn't be ignored that the prices were double what they'd once been—even if they were still cheaper than all the other new restaurants in Logan Square. It wasn't uncommon for people to walk in and scoff, for the neighborhood's unhoused population to panhandle from the brunch crowd. Weekday mornings, we would serve Latinx families, construction workers of all races, suburban whites, hipster theatre kids, mothers with their young toddlers, and those who just needed a cup of coffee sitting side by side at the diner counter. I loved our clientele. There was an ease between the staff and guests, which was partially due to the tone set by the chef and the manager. Sarah would call friendly greetings to regulars that she liked, snap at guests who thought the food was taking too long (which ruled), and when she had time, interact with kids hanging out with their parents. Jessie believed that hospitality was how you made people feel, so the staff was given free rein to be ourselves and make them feel how we might want if the situation was reversed. After my time waiting tables, I liked breaking down the artifice that comes from so much restaurant work. In a hyper-segregated city, it didn't escape notice that Johnny's had created a small integrated space, but in the end, none of that would save the neighborhood from continuing its path of gentrification. None of that would make it easier for the city's vulnerable communities to live.

That summer, I'd rise early the mornings I worked, sometimes before dawn, my body aching, my mind blurry. Without showering (there was no point), I'd hop on my bike. As the sun rose, I'd pedal from Pilsen, a neighborhood undergoing its own challenging transformation of which I was, once again, complicit. I'd maneuver along side streets and parking lots, through the medical district and onto the West Side, over the Eisenhower, past industrial warehouses and residential streets. The West Side was changing too, connecting the development of the West Loop to Garfield Park, still in its early stages of gentrification. I saw shiny condo buildings and white families with strollers in places I knew they hadn't been for many decades. I'd zip through Humboldt Park and remember when it had once been considered dangerous, that as a young post-grad new to the city, I'd been told never to go there. But now that neighborhood was transforming, into something shinier but not greater. I wondered if the whole city was like this, everything changing, already changed, about to change, the whole city churning and shifting and dying and burning and building back up, but I loved the city, sometimes more than I ever thought possible, more than I probably deserved. I couldn't actually believe that I was leaving, couldn't fathom what I'd do once I got to where I was going, and knowing somehow that I was doomed from the jump, that I'd always want to come back to the only place as an adult that I ever really thought to call home.

I did return to Chicago, a year after I left. I didn't return to work at Johnny's or live in Logan Square. One visit on a weekend morning told me all I needed to know: it had slowed down. The shine had worn off. The customers weren't clamoring to get in, and no local magazines were running adulatory reviews of the food, which was still very good. The media had moved on.

Johnny's closed for good in the fall of 2017. The space on the corner of the square is home to a swanky cocktail bar with long windows called Young American, itself closed due to coronavirus and pivoted to Big Kids Chicago, a takeout joint serving sandwiches as big as a head. Inside, I can see shadows of Johnny's and the Mezcaleria. A big open space with neon lighting, the new bar sticks out in the neighborhood, incongruous for those of us who knew what it once looked like. But in five years, will anyone remember? In five years, Young American or Big Kids or whatever it is next may look like it's been there forever or not be there at all.

What Else Do You Do?

At the end of my shift, the head of the table I was serving stopped talking to his guests and signaled to me with a hand. "So, Nick," he asked, with little apparent malice, "what else do you do?"

My stomach dropped. I hate this question. Every server I know hates this question. If I'm feeling empathetic, if I'm doing my job, I'll respond honestly. But that January night was rainy and gross outside, and my final table—that table—was keeping me an hour past the end of my shift, so I was cagey. I leaned back on the balls of my feet, gave them a little shrug, and said: "I make dinner. See movies. Read books."

At home, I seethed. "How dare they ask me that question," I said to my girlfriend. "I don't walk into their doctor's office and ask them what else they do with their life."

Nicholas Ward

I took to the internet. "Fellow servers," I wrote on Facebook, "how do you respond to the 'What else do you do?' question?"

Antonio, a longtime Chicago server friend, responded first: "Tersely," he said. "Usually with a smug look on my face. 'Travel, explore food culture, enjoy my freedom, cherish being my own boss, and taking time for me when I want.'"

Katie, whom I once cast in a play, summed it up nicely: "I usually make a wounded face and say something like: 'Oh. Are you . . . are you saying a job in hospitality isn't real?' I think it embarrasses them and makes them feel guilty for insulting me."

"Why are you so worked up?" my girlfriend asked. "You do tons of other things. You could have just told them."

She's right. I worked at twenty different restaurants between 1998 and 2018, and I always had a side hustle. My first few years in Chicago I worked like mad, bouncing from joint to joint while breaking into the city's theatre scene.

I guess the real issue was that I was worried I wasn't living my life correctly. I made enough money but never socked anything away for an emergency. I retained health insurance on and off but rarely went to the doctor, even when I needed to. I plunged excess income into bars, cabs I took to get home, cigarettes I tried like hell to quit. When I got the "what else do you do?" question back then, it was always the same people asking: white men who were my father's age range and type—middle-class Midwesterners—whom I suspected saw a bit of their offspring in me. Often, I was happy to answer: "I'm an actor/producer/ please god get me out of this industry."

I told myself I'd have to leave the restaurant industry someday, but I failed to imagine what I'd leave it for. I didn't want office work. I didn't possess other skills. Make it in theatre or wait tables forever: those felt like the only two options.

I see now that I let my middle-class anxiety taint how I once felt about restaurants. I'm a white kid raised in the suburbs by public school teachers who retired with sound financial prospects. I earned a college degree. I thought all this meant I wasn't supposed to spend my life waiting tables. But I made money doing so, sometimes really good money, sometimes more than I've made anywhere else. And I enjoyed doing it.

Of course, not all servers are treated equally. My body wasn't sexualized and harassed daily; I never had any physical challenges that prevented me from being on my feet for eight hours at a time, sometimes more. And I often only needed to work one restaurant job to survive. Most food service workers aren't quite so lucky: there are nine million restaurant workers in this country, many of whom earn very low wages. The COVID-19 pandemic has wreaked further havoc on an industry that already treated people as disposable—adding mass layoffs, unsafe working conditions, and a wave of independent business closures to the preexisting issues of lack of healthcare, rising food costs, battles over the future of tipping, and a fight for $15 labor advocacy that dares to suggest that all people deserve to earn a living wage. That I'm not in the muck of it all is a matter of lucky breaks, a college degree, and my previous job at a prestigious theatre. My own anxieties about my life in the industry are a pittance compared to the concerns of workers I spent most of my life working alongside, who all deserved better. Everyone deserves so much better.

When I worked at Steppenwolf, I missed the action. Sure, I had stability: a salary, a predictable schedule, paid vacation days, a 401(k), and a small role in creating some of the finest art in the world. But office life held no allure for me. That I was able to choose between one and the other was a privilege not lost on me. Most people in either industry don't get to make that choice.

One Sunday night, I helped an old coworker throw a party at

Nicholas Ward

a house in Oak Park. He'd organized a pop-up event, pairing a chef with a local host for an elegant dinner in a unique setting. On a brisk October evening, with no room inside the house, we washed dishes in the moonlight, drying plates just in time for the next course. It was fun and silly. We laughed, giddy. I didn't have one single moment like that working at a theatre.

When I left Steppenwolf after three years, I dove back into the restaurant world with a ferocity only matched by my first years out of college. I worked at Freds Chicago at Barneys New York, located in Chicago's Gold Coast; I spent a year and a half at a Michelin-starred fine-dining restaurant before moving on to Johnny's Grill. I was seven restaurants deep in my post-Steppenwolf life before landing another nonprofit arts job and leaving the industry for good. Maybe. I always said that I would never say never to going back. But after COVID, I don't know how much there's going to be to go back to.

As I got older, The Question started to take on a different tone. I look younger than my age and worked for a spell near a local university. People probably thought I was a student marking time. They were surprised when I told them my age, when I told them serving was my profession. There was a tinge of concern in their faces, as if I somehow failed their expectations, as if I "deserved more than this."

It's fine that those folks took an interest in my life. But I can't help but wonder if they were equally as curious about the cooks who make the food they're eating? The folks in back washing dishes? The various silent assistants clearing plates and bringing their food? Did they find value in their backstory, those coworkers of mine who often don't look like me? If the clientele who can afford to dine at the restaurants where I've worked saw all of us as people who deserved more, would they be willing to pay more for their meal and, by doing so, help drive up wages for all? Or was I the only one deserving of their attention?

136

What I know is that the restaurant industry is complicated and multi-faceted, with a host of problems as indicative of our country as any other industry: not enough maternity leave, no paternity leave, high rates of sexual harassment, racial segregation, and labor violations. I know that my success in this field is due in part to the privileges afforded by my identity. Still, I was happy to stay in the game as long as I did and grateful that I was mostly surrounded by decent people, rather than pretend it wasn't a career.

I Can Always Be Found

Year Zero

Prologue

We came from Ohio in a caravan. Matt's old pickup fishtailed on the highway; Will navigated the U-Haul; my cat howled in terror in the passenger seat of my '99 Saturn; Betsy lumbered along in her minivan with her own (tranquilized) feline. We unloaded the cars in the blistering August heat, cursing as we coaxed Betsy's inflexible wood-framed couches around the stairwell of our new walk-up. Stefanie—the South Suburbs native—showed up late and lifted nothing. In her defense, she organized painting the apartment before we all arrived. We searched for dinner up and down Milwaukee Avenue, five suburban-raised white kids in a Latinx neighborhood searching for the perfect meal to start our new lives.

Nicholas Ward

Later, we'd rhapsodize about this night, our first in Chicago, imagining and bestowing a grandiosity on it that didn't match the actual evening.

We settled on Abríl, the Mexican joint that gazed into the heart of our new neighborhood. It wouldn't survive the gentrification lurking along Logan Square's edges, but we didn't know that then. Nor did we understand how we would contribute to that.

We were sweaty and tired and irritable with each other. The drive had taken longer than expected because Will went straight through Indianapolis when I told him to take the highway around the outskirts of the city, and Betsy cried every five minutes, it seemed, because Stef was pissed at her for putting the gas bill in her name. But Betsy had no credit, so the company made us wait two weeks for service, which meant we had no hot water. I had less than a hundred dollars to my name and really shouldn't have been splurging on dinner out, and Matt was all bummed because we picked a not-very-good restaurant for our first meal. To cap it off, our new apartment on the second floor of a two-flat building was filled, floor-to-ceiling, with all the crap we'd packed from an idyllic house in a college town four times that size.

Lost in our menus and our silent frustration, we didn't notice someone stagger over from the bar. My friends still swear he wasn't older than thirty-five, but I recall him as ancient: lines in his face weathered like grooves in a slab of rock, eyebrows bushy. He bent over and fixed his gaze on Will. Everyone stopped talking.

The man pulled out a driver's license and held it up to my friend's face.

"Hello," Will said. He tried his best to seem polite, but his eyes were uneasy. Betsy bowed her head to stare at the floor, tears streaming silently down her cheeks. She grabbed Will's hand and buried her face in his shoulder.

Frozen to my chair, I watched the man point to the picture on his own ID and then slide closer to my friend.

"You," he said, pointing a finger at Will. "You are going to die in five years."

Commotion ensued. Betsy burst into fresh tears; Matt shot up but realized he couldn't do anything and sat back down. The man pushed his ID closer to Will's stony face as a waitress barreled out of the kitchen to snap at him and force him away from us.

We finished our meal in silence. No one wanted to admit how scared we all were, how sheltered we'd been as kids, the ease with which we'd lived our lives. After dinner, we smoked cigarettes on the sidewalk outside the restaurant. Betsy clung to Will, tears still rolling down her cheeks. In front of us, a traffic circle spun around a small green park. A car stopped at the light, two dudes blaring music. The guy on the passenger side tapped the driver and pointed at Betsy, laughing as they sped off up Milwaukee Avenue. Sobs again.

I wanted to sneer at my friends, at their sadness and anxiety. Were they really so unprepared for the harsh realities of adulthood? Of the city? And if they were, what did that mean for me?

Summer

My second week, I waltzed across Kedzie Boulevard for an interview as an assistant manager at Lula, a cramped and funky restaurant full of mismatched tables and local art. Logan Square in 2004 was mostly family-owned Mexican and Afro-Caribbean joints, dive bars, and greasy spoons; to my eyes, Lula Cafe looked like a step down from The Alexander House, Oxford, Ohio's finest white-tablecloth establishment, where I'd served for two years in college. I had no idea that Lula was a serious-minded business that shifted expertly between simple and refined farm-to-table food, that it would eventually become a flagship destination for the neighborhood and the city. I figured I could stroll right in and be offered a job on the spot.

"Theatre major, huh?" the co-owner asked when we sat down. "That going to interfere with your ability to work the floor? We can't have you ditching out for a last-minute audition."

"No, sir, I don't plan on pursuing theatre anytime soon." I wanted to cut my teeth on restaurant work and figure out the city that way. He would've had a right to ask why I put theatre on my resume in the first place.

"How's your Spanish?" he continued.

"I understand better than I speak," I lied. With no high school or college language requirement, I hadn't bothered with it.

"Okay." He adjusted his glasses. "What's kohlrabi?"

"I'm sorry?"

"Kohlrabi. Explain kohlrabi to me. Do you know it?"

I racked my brain. Had we served it at The Alexander House? Had I eaten it before? Was it food?

"Uh, it's, like, uh, similar to a pomegranate."

"Actually," he said, "it's a perennial vegetable more closely related to cabbage. And it's delicious. But don't worry, you can be taught."

I didn't get the job.

I didn't get hired at Lucca on Southport and Diversey.

Or Joe's Stone Crab on Grand Avenue, just north of the river.

"I keep hearing how hard it is for graduates to find employment," my dad said, referring to the first whispers of the recession that would take hold four years later.

"How do you explain that all of my friends have jobs already?" I asked.

Like so:

Stefanie transferred from the Starbucks in Evergreen Park, Illinois, to the one by our house.

Betsy's fancy talent agency out in Schaumburg hired a wave of recent grads.

Will's boss at the Wicker Park Half & Half thought he was attractive.

Matt's homegrown cooking chops secured him a spot on the line at Spring, a three-star restaurant.

It was a crapshoot.

"Do you need us to send you any money?" my mom asked.

I didn't want them to. I couldn't assert my independence, make my own way, if I borrowed money from my mom and dad. Nevertheless, one hundred dollars wasn't going to last until the end of my second week.

"Let's see how it goes," I said.

I scoured Chicago, discovering my new city but one that merely encompassed a few square miles of the Near North Side. I traveled from the Loop, where the buildings loomed as tall as giants, all the way north to Wrigley Field, where the Cubs were in the process of blowing a promising season just one year after an epic collapse. I took elevated trains that snaked through Lincoln Park and Old Town, buses straight along the city's grid system; I walked for blocks along Damen and Milwaukee and North Avenues in Wicker Park and Bucktown. I fell in love with the city day by day, moment by moment, returning home each afternoon elated but defeated.

I couldn't find work: not with French haute cuisine nor at restaurants featuring inspired tasting menus, not in traditional fine-dining places nor upscale burger joints, not at neighborhood staples, downtown seafood and steak restaurants, Asian fusion restaurants, restaurants that would close within the year, long-standing establishments, places I love to this day, and some I flat-out despise. Not a single one required my services. With each rejection, each unreturned phone call, I felt waves of shame roll over me. Could I really not find a fucking job as a waiter? All I wanted was to begin adulthood, free of the restraints of adolescence: no class schedules or homework or anybody dictating how to structure my life, just me and the unknowable future, filled with possibility. But at every turn, Chicago slammed the door on all I envisioned for myself.

Nicholas Ward

But there's also this: I did not apply to gas stations, liquor stores, coffee shops, all-night diners, bookstores, retail chains, franchise restaurants, or temp agencies. I didn't apply to bartend at a theatre, pouring crap wine and restocking coffee. I didn't apply to be a busser or a runner in any of the restaurants I applied to be a server at, and a few of them even asked. I sought entrance into a world I didn't understand and expected to immediately ascend into its upper echelon. Probably I felt like I'd earned it—with my one job at the one fine-dining place in my college town. I definitely felt I deserved it—I'd spent my entire life cloistered inside the middle-class and refused to relinquish that status anytime soon. Maybe, in the back of my mind somewhere, I understood the net would catch me, that it would never let me fall too hard.

Football season started, and I still didn't have a job. The Bush vs. Kerry election inched closer, but I was unengaged. What did a presidential election matter when I couldn't find work? I possessed all the privilege and access the world had to offer, and I took it for granted. Eventually, I borrowed money from my parents, money that paid the rent, that bought me groceries, that kept me going in my quest.

At least I had my friends and our apartment. The five of us, plus two cats and a hamster, were stuffed into a four-bedroom in Logan Square. It was everything I'd envisioned from city living: We'd sit out on the front stoop and smoke cigarettes or drink wine in the backyard; we'd chat amicably with our neighbors when we saw them, with our landlords who lived across the street. Sometimes we'd stroll the boulevards, where the city had preserved remnants of the historic linking of parks, and marvel at the Gothic- and Tudor-style homes now broken up into apartments—mansions compared to the two- and three-flats that lined our street. Weekends that summer and early fall were filled with picnics and cookouts, children laughing and playing, music from all corners of the earth. A saxophonist practiced, and on hot, sunny days, we'd open the windows and let the sounds of the city waft into our apartment.

Fall

On October 4, almost two months to the day from our arrival, I applied for a serving job at Cy's Crab House on Ashland Avenue in Wrigleyville. A hulking structure framed by high windows and corporate beer signs, I'd driven past Cy's a few times and avoided it on general principle. Its kitschy aura was the furthest place I wanted to land. But I was desperate and without any job prospects.

A woman seated at the bar, pouring over stacks of papers, greeted me. "Good afternoon. Here for lunch?" She was in her late thirties, glasses perched on her nose, long flowing black hair, trace of a lilting British accent. The restaurant was otherwise empty.

"No," I said, "I'm here about the serving job."

"Fill this out, please," she said, smiling and handing me an application.

I took a seat at the bar and absorbed the seafaring motif: gangplanks, ships' wheels, hanging ropes, and stuffed sharks next to Cubs' banners, flat-screen TVs, and the specials board written in faded chalk. For a brief moment, I thought about fleeing: my parents could support me for a little while longer, and eventually, some place "appropriate" was bound to hire me. But no, that wouldn't do. It was time to grow up.

"I'm Sahar, one of the managers," the woman said when I returned the completed application. "Can you start tomorrow?"

"Tomorrow?" I repeated. Was I getting a job? "Yeah. Yes. Of course."

"Ten a.m., please. Black pants, black shoes, black shirt. See you then."

On the way home, I called my parents, my roommates, anyone who'd been following my saga, screaming the good news into the phone. Tempering myself, I wondered if I got lucky on that particular day, catching Sahar in a moment of obvious weakness.

It was a strange restaurant. Up front, with the pirate-themed decorations, the dining room was crammed with tables that were barely occupied but impossible to pass through when they were. The back half was carpeted and austere but kept dark and closed most of the time. Servers wrote and processed all checks by hand, and the kitchen operated at the very end of the building, so the entire enterprise—ringing in food, retrieving an extra condiment, refilling coffee—meant a full minute and a half off the floor. The staff was bitter about getting too few shifts for too little money and spent most of the time smoking in the side break station. I soon resented having to take two buses to get there, being forced to dress up for Halloween, and enduring the cruel owners, who sat and read the paper while stuffing their faces with food we served them for no gratuity.

But I was grateful for Sahar. Overworked and criticized on all sides by the servers and managers, she remained calm, never losing her patience with anyone. I'll always appreciate what she did for me, even though it may have meant nothing for her. She helped me get a foothold in this city, ensuring I didn't have to move home, that I didn't have to give up.

Once I got my first job, I pulled my head out of the sand to discover that the first two months had been hell for my friends, too.

Will woke up five days a week at 5 a.m. to serve coffee to commuters; he took a short afternoon nap, spent a few hours each night with Betsy, before he slept and repeated. He was miserable, hating everything—Logan Square, the CTA, the Bears, the traffic—the whole city that I was growing to love.

Betsy had an even rougher time. Almost a month to the day after we moved, her cousin died in a car accident. Around that time, she also discovered that the fancy job she'd gotten her first week, as a talent agent at John Robert Powers, was entirely commission-based and cloaked cold calling. We spent our "fun-employment" together watching *Queer Eye for the Straight Guy*. I didn't know it at the time, but she was terrified. Navigating the city, making new friends, even the simple act of living somewhere new, scared the crap out of her.

Matt's spot on the line at a three-star restaurant quickly went down in flames, too. After one particularly stressful shift (I never got the full story from him, so I'm not totally sure how accurate this is), his boss told him he was fucking up and that he needed to step up. Matt packed his knives and never looked back. Shortly thereafter, he ended up working in some capacity for the archdiocese and his future father-in-law, Stefanie's dad. We joked about this hypocrisy, a lapsed Catholic working for the overlords while he lived in sin with his girlfriend. They maintained separate rooms in the apartment, dressing down Matt's unused bedroom to appear lived-in whenever relatives visited to hide the fact that they spent every night together.

Only Stefanie seemed above the fray somehow. She worked at the Starbucks down the street, took classes at Second City, never struggled with paying rent or bills or finding her way, but maybe that's because she already knew the city a bit from growing up along its outskirts.

It was a tense situation. Our big, beautiful four-bedroom turned small once we inhabited it. Thin walls meant that any mild fighting or fucking resonated throughout the apartment. Zeta, Betsy's cat, routinely terrorized Amadeus, my cat, by chasing him throughout the apartment, the two howling and hissing while we all tried to sleep. Matt hated that Betsy made her cat wear a bell, Will hated that Matt wanted to get a dog, I hated that Will bitched about the city so much, everybody hated how loudly I played my music, Stefanie seemed to pick fights with Matt, Will and Betsy seemed on the verge of breaking up, and I felt like the repository for all my friends' personal relationship squabbles.

Nicholas Ward

We survived it somehow. Almost two decades after we moved to Chicago together, we are family. I've been in their weddings and broken bread at their kids' christenings—I feel more connected to them than many of my actual blood relatives. That first year, when none of us knew what the fuck we were doing, a missed utility bill or a sarcastic remark about whose turn it was to take out the garbage could have ruptured the fault lines of our friendships permanently. In the end, nothing came between us. I'm still not entirely sure how that happened.

Winter

I slumped on the clean couch; Will stood over me after his morning shift.

"You have to tell Betsy," he said.

"She's gonna be really pissed."

He nodded. "Probably." He glanced at the stained couch across the living room and removed his scarf. "Dude, just call her."

I dialed Betsy at work, where she'd found employment as a receptionist for an insurance company.

"Betsy . . . I pissed on your couch last night."

It started in December after I'd been hired as a server at Nacional 27.

To celebrate my first night on the floor, Matt met me out at Nick's Beer Garden in Wicker Park. It was a Thursday. Matt, too, had moved jobs again, from the archdiocese to waiting tables at a bar and grill in Old Town.

We got so drunk that night, the kind of outlandish statement drunk, our-futures-crystallizing-in-front-of-our-eyes drunk. We got so drunk that we were separated on the way home. Matt, never one for directions, somehow didn't follow me onto the train back to Logan Square but instead got on the one headed for downtown and then got back off, and instead of just going home, he kept circling the streets of Wicker Park looking for me, calling my name, calling my cell phone—which I had conveniently left at home.

When he finally came home, he told me he'd been going up to people on the street and asking them if they'd seen me. "'He's worth a quarter-of-a-million dollars!' I screamed," he slurred later.

Betsy laughed, sitting near us on the couch. "That's not a lot of money, actually," she said ruefully because, while that was true, it was a fortune to us.

Later that night, I stumbled out of my room and over to the coffee table, lifted the front cover of the nearest book like the lid of a toilet seat, and pissed all over it.

"What are you doing?" Matt asked from the hallway, in the midst of his own sojourn to the bathroom.

"I'm peeing." Like it was the most obvious thing in the world.

The next morning, in the crusty glow of my hangover, Matt burst out from his room to gleefully recount my escapades. When Will came home at noon, he told the story again. And again when Stefanie returned at 2 p.m. And once more when Betsy arrived at 6 p.m. We all had a good healthy laugh about it, me included, while Betsy and Stefanie reenacted the story until it reached vaudevillian proportions.

The next week, I went out for a few beers with my new coworkers and urinated in the hallway by the bathroom. The week after that, I piddled in my cat's litter box.

All that winter—through the holidays and New Year's, whether two beers or ten—at least once a week, when my bladder called, I couldn't control my feet. Each morning, I had zero recollections of the incident. I was only conscious for the aftermath, when I discovered the location of the stain. In my shoes. In my sweater drawer. On Betsy's couch.

"It's not funny anymore, Nick."

"I know."

"I'll try to find the company that made the couch," she said. "But you need to get help."

Nicholas Ward

"I will," I said.

I felt shame about asking someone else for help. But I couldn't solve the problem on my own. At the health center in our neighborhood, the doctor suggested I set an alarm for the middle of each night, to wake myself up and use the bathroom. It was something so simple, a way to trick my body into complying with my demands. But it worked.

Spring

Will and Betsy moved out on a sunny and bright afternoon in April. They were only moving two streets west and two streets north, but it felt like we'd be worlds apart. We hadn't been but a few steps away from each other for a whole year.

When I asked Will why they were moving, he said with a shrug, "We wanna have sex with the door open." Which meant: "We're ready to start our life together."

Will and Betsy had spoken lovingly about their new apartment: a backyard with a fire pit, landlords just a few years older who lived above them. They invited us over as soon as they got everything set up. None of us had a clue where our lives were going, but we knew we'd be there together. All we had to do was show up.

We milled around on the front stoop saying our goodbyes.

"I'll miss you," Stefanie said.

"We're right over there," Betsy said with a nod of her head.

"I know," Stefanie said. "But still."

Will and Matt and I spoke in hushed, secretive tones, smoking cigarettes on the stoop. It was exactly how we'd met almost five years prior on the first day of our freshman year at Miami University.

"You'll text us when it's done?" I asked Will.

"Of course," he said, looking over his shoulder at Betsy.

"It'll be great," Matt said. Will was planning to propose to Betsy that night, with a ring he had bought at Target. In the absence of any saved income, it was an offering, a symbol for their future.

We said our final goodbyes and exchanged hugs.

A *pop-pop-pop* echoed from down the block. We watched as a car wheeled down our street and gunned past us. For a second, no one spoke.

"Was that a drive-by?" I asked.

"I think so," Matt said.

"Anyone get a look?" Will asked.

No one had. No one remembered the car or the driver. And as far as I know, none of us called the police.

It wasn't the first gunfire we'd heard. A few days prior, during a 2-a.m. stillness, I sat in bed reading, Matt was in the backyard smoking, and similar noises ruptured our quietude. Later, we heard rumors that people had died on both occasions, that the violence stemmed from a drug dealer's house on the corner, whatever that meant. However close this was to our doorstep, we never felt unsafe. We felt the violence in our neighborhood lived in a different world than we did, that we could always move away if it got too close. We co-opted the space for our own needs without investing in the actual community. None of us bought homes there; none of us put down roots; none of us live there anymore.

Coda

Will and Betsy lived in Logan Square the longest, their time stretched over four apartments. Once they dreamed of owning a home there, but they were eventually forced north to Lincoln Square, following in the footsteps of many an office worker/ theatre artist couple. Matt and Stefanie became Chicago schoolteachers, bought a house in Beverly in 2010, gave birth to Greta a year later, moved to Cleveland for a spell, and then back to Beverly again, baby Eleanor in tow. They now have three children after welcoming Paul into their life.

Abril became a restaurant called Reno, all bagel sandwiches and Stumptown coffee. It's the perfect spot to write on a weekday morning, looking out on all that Logan Square has become—the community garden and commissioned street art and bustling white faces—and remember how it used to be.

I moved all over Chicago, to Roscoe Village for a half decade, then back to Logan for two years, to Pilsen for a spell, then Bridgeport, before finally settling on the North Side again. I've seen gentrification blossom almost everywhere I put my feet. In Pilsen, a record store opened the week I moved there. A new coffee shop got tagged with anti-gentrification graffiti. A contentious mixed-use space called Thalia Hall has become an institution for all the new arrivals. Like them, I benefitted from, and contributed to, the shifting demographics of the neighbor-hood. But I don't know how much my awareness meant then, or now. I think about all the others just like me: artists and bartenders and graphic designers, new graduates of Midwest universities, fresh-faced young white kids trying to get a foothold in the city of their dreams, a place they don't understand at all.

Paul and Patti and Me

Many nights, too many to count, it was just us.

We'd sit in the backyard, in a semi-circle of lawn chairs off the enclosed porch. We'd stare at the rows of vegetables, the old barn, the long-defunct chicken coop, all the details of Paul's old farmhouse that I will never forget. From inside came the soft folk music from his mom's record player, but otherwise it would be quiet, the other houses on Paul's street tucking into bed long before. Patti would hug her legs up to her chest, her wild, curly red hair falling around her while she rested her head against the cool tin of the chair. I'd light a cigarette, scratch my scalp—teasing out my hair from the gel I overapplied each morning. Paulie would bring out a guitar passed down from his grandfather and strum. It was the summer after our junior year of high school, 1999, the new millennium fast approaching, the heat exploding in our hometown.

"Today was perfect," Paul said one night, head bent towards the ground, fingers picking the strings, lips pursed, searching for the right chord.

I smiled, flicked the ashes off my smoke. That afternoon, we'd picked up Patti from her job at the Farmington Bakery for a jaunt to Flipside Records in Clawson, scouring the racks for buried treasure. After we made our purchases, we climbed back in Paulie's white Ford Probe and hopped on the freeway. Paul drove; a mixtape played, the drone of Galaxie 500's guitar washing over us as we cruised well past our hometown through an unchanging landscape of overpasses and rest stations, no destination in mind. We had no commitments, no jobs or dinners with parents to get home to, so Paul kept on driving. Patti sifted through the stacks of magazines he kept in his car, warm summer air blowing her hair around and all over the backseat. I stared out the window at the fading sun as we played tape after tape, waves of sound crashing around me.

Back at his house, Paul's plucking became recognizable, transforming into that famous Jeff Buckley cover of "Hallelujah."

Patti sat up, alert, lifting her shoulders from their calm repose and hunching over to stare at him. I'd seen Paul play music before: strumming bass in his middle school band, trading guitar riffs with a friend in his brother's basement apartment, on the piano at the top of the stairs of that old farmhouse. But that night, under the bright Michigan stars, the magic he coaxed from his fingertips circled the three of us, binding us together forever. I felt a sense of contentment, of being completely full, overwhelm me. It rose outward from my stomach, up through my sternum, exploding in my chest and tingling down through my shoulders to my arms, my hands, my fingers, and then shooting into the ground. That was what I needed in my life, and I mourned the sixteen years spent without Patti and Paul. Maybe I knew then that what we had was fleeting, that none of us could stay in that place together forever. I caught Patti wiping the tears that rolled down her cheeks. Maybe she knew it too.

Paulie finished the song and we exhaled together. I hadn't realized I had been holding my breath.

"Wow," Patti said softly.

Paul responded with a nod. "I'm glad you're both here."

Patti smiled. "Me too," she said.

We didn't speak much the rest of that night. Paul, it seemed, had said it all.

Eight years later, Patti and I stand in the same backyard, far enough away from the house not to be seen. We share a bottle of cheap chardonnay and a pack of Parliament Lights as the snow falls in the darkness. Everything has changed for us. I live in Chicago now, Patti in Los Angeles, and we're home for the holidays, swigging shitty wine and staring at Paul's old house.

Just two years ago tonight. The night that Paul died by suicide.

"You know," I say, passing the bottle back over to Patti. "Paul didn't really like you when he first met you. He thought you were too familiar, had too much energy, didn't really listen."

"Bitchface," Patti says loudly, invoking her pet name for me, "you never told me that."

I shrug. "Maybe he fell in love with you at first sight and didn't know what to do."

Patti goes silent. I have to remind myself that we're talking about her fiancé, not merely our best friend from high school.

A light flicks on inside the house, and I take a step back.

"It's fine," Patti says. "Nobody can see us back here. Besides, they're not coming outside tonight."

Paul's family is probably inside alone, mourning his passing in their own way. He didn't commit the act in the house itself, but my guess is that the ghost of Paul still lingers there.

"We made a great team," Patti says.

I don't know if she means just her and Paul, or me and her and Paul, but either way, I agree.

I met Paul Myers in the first grade when I sat down in Ms. Delaney's class and asked the chubby kid behind me, the one gazing out the window at the playground, what animal he had on his shirt. Without dropping focus from the jungle gym, Paul whispered, "Meerkats."

Everything about Paul illuminated my own deficiencies. He was a great baseball player; I barely made contact. His family lived on a farm where they raised chickens; I lived in a subdivision. He wore thrift store T-shirts at seven years old, which seemed cool even then, like Paulie woke up each morning with his own sense of style. I was dressed by my mom.

The first time he came over to my house, he brought a boombox and asked, "Do you like to dance?" We spent the few hours before my parents called us to dinner dancing to Kylie Minogue's "Locomotion" in my basement.

He was my first real friend. As the only child of two working parents, I grew up around other kids, spent afternoons after school at houses in the subdivision. But all those people were thrust upon me. I chose Paul. When Patti came along, we'd been friends for eleven years, weaving in and out and back into each other's lives.

Patricia Wheeler—Patti for short—moved to Farmington with her parents and two younger siblings at the beginning of junior year, where she hooked up with the Goth kids. Paul and I knew them as a quiet and friendly group, harmless despite the black trench coats, eye makeup, and painted fingernails. Patti wore flannel shirts but was forever in their company.

It was early December 1998, a Wednesday, when word surfaced about Mike Heller, a sophomore in their set. Mike was a boisterous kid we'd gone to school with since the second grade. I remember that morning vividly: Paul and I stood at our lockers across from the teachers' lounge. We watched smoke seep out behind the cracks of the closed door, curl around the handle, dance into the crowded hallway.

"What the hell?" Paul asked. Students crisscrossed on their way to first period. Few of them took notice.

"You didn't hear?" I asked Paul. "Mike Heller killed himself."

Paul held his eyes on the closed door. He had shot up past me, dwarfing me by five inches. With his constant stubble, long sideburns, perfectly coiffed curly hair, he looked like a man in his twenties—while I remained a boy in my teens.

The bell rang. We didn't move.

"They're letting them smoke in there," Paul said. "That's smart."

I nodded, thinking that Mike's friends needed a safe space to smoke and cry together.

The door opened and they filed out, clinging to each other as they shuffled to class. Patti, hair pulled back, eyes puffy behind her glasses, saw us and peeled off from the group. I threw my backpack down and gave her a big, silent hug. She moved on to Paul, who bent down to give her an awkward squeeze.

"Okay," Patti said, straightening, wiping her eyes, steeling herself for the day in a manner I would see again later. "Time to go to class."

"Who is that?" Paul asked after she was clear.

"Patti Wheeler," I replied.

"You're friends?" he asked.

"Yeah, I guess. I don't really know her, but she gives lots of hugs."

Paulie frowned. "I think maybe she's in my English class and I've never noticed her."

Later that year, as all the juniors were saying their summer goodbyes, Patti asked me, "Can we hang out this summer? I need new friends."

Things had spiraled into chaos for the Goths after Mike Heller's death, fueled by drinking and blaming each other for his suicide. I told Patti she could come along with us any Saturday she wanted, to go record shopping and drive around. I'd moved crews a lot in high school. First, I hung with the preppy kids, then with Kurt, Ryan, and Jonny when that fizzled out. When they betrayed me, or I betrayed them, I needed a soft place to land.

We became a team, a fortress against the outside world. No girlfriends or boyfriends or parents or the future could get in. We were Nick and Paul and Patti, together always: homecoming, football games, parties, the hallway at school. It was Patti's kitchen floor where I cried about girls, smoking pot in Paul's old barn and listening to his fears of getting older, the all-night diner by the highway where we took Patti for cheesy fries the night she broke up with her boyfriend. We made a literary magazine together and even produced two plays. But by the time senior year wound down, we had our sights set on the holy grail: The Talent Show.

"We gotta do something," I told them. "It's our ritual." Paul and I were veterans of two previous high school talent shows, but this one needed to be special.

"I want in," Patti said. "I wanna leave everyone with a lasting impression."

It was April, graduation was on the horizon, three different universities awaiting our arrival shortly after that. I was off to school at Miami of Ohio, a public school halfway between Cincinnati and Dayton, near the Indiana border—five whole hours southwest of our hometown. Paul and Patti, meanwhile, would be at Eastern Michigan and Michigan State, a stone's throw away from each other. I didn't know it at the time, but the talent show was to be our last hurrah.

We had cut AP English that day; our circle in the backyard was the best option for hashing out our act for the three-hour spectacle that sent the entire student body nutty with anticipation.

"But what are we going to do?" Patti asked.

We shifted our focus to Paul. He sat silently, one leg crossed over the other, thrift store cardigan hanging from his frame. He was so cool. He smoothed his hands over his forehead, up through his dirty blond hair.

"We shall play a song, of course," he said. "Patticakes, I will teach you bass; you'll only need three chords. Nick, as before, we'll use your serviceable set of pipes. I'll play lead guitar," he paused for effect, taking a sharp drag off a cigarette, "and we will leave this town in a blaze of motherfucking glory."

We couldn't achieve this without Paul's guidance. And it wasn't just that he played instruments and we didn't. Paulie had swagger. If he said we could do it, we were going do it.

Patti asked The Question. "What song?" Music was everything to us, our language and philosophy, our religion and worship, and Paul was our prophet. While most kids in our high school were just discovering Zeppelin or The Smashing Pumpkins, Paul guided us to bootlegged Prince, to Sonic Youth turned way up. Paul would have the answer.

"Alice Cooper," Paul responded. "'I'm Eighteen.' That's our jam."

It was an odd choice. At that time, Alice Cooper was known more for his absurd cameo in *Wayne's World*, not the anti-establishment rebel of his heyday. But goddamn, that song felt like us. We were eighteen. We were confused every day. We had to get out of this place.

One night, after a chaotic and sweaty rehearsal, Paul said, "We're going to transcend everything: this show, this town, our lives. I hope you guys are ready."

The stage at our school was a gigantic proscenium that opened onto a five-hundred-person house, and that night, it was packed with students, parents, and teachers. We began in total darkness. A spotlight popped center to unveil our trio. I wore skintight leather pants and a maroon halter top, my arms held aloft, fingers extended into twin devil horns, the rock 'n' roll salute. To my right, Paulie slouched like a '50s beatnik behind his 1994 40th Anniversary Edition Midnight-Blue Fender Stratocaster, a kilt around his waist and pantyhose on his head. Patti posed to my left, suited up for the bass guitar in a brightly colored apron worn over a bikini. The lights rose to reveal Tom, leader of the Goths, hunched over a drum set, and Grant, the captain of the football team, on rhythm guitar with a turquoise shirt and painted fingernails. Before we even began, our fellow classmates went batshit crazy.

Paulie pealed off a disgusting riff, cruising into "I'm Eighteen," and the rest of us blasted off. I threw myself around like a man on fire, screaming the lyrics with joy; Tom banged the drumsticks with fury and abandon; Patti preened and pranced; and Grant broke a string and fuzzed out for the whole song. And Paul? Deliberately, furiously, purposefully, he ripped off all of the strings on that blue beauty and the stage exploded in noise. To top it all off, there was a fucking smoke machine.

I have watched this performance many times on VHS, and it wasn't perfect. The mix was a mess, the bass and drums were out of sync, and I couldn't sing nearly as well as I thought. But never in the history of the Great Lakes did three friends make rock 'n' roll purer, rowdier, and freer than we did that night. Picture the stage smothered in fog, too-hot white lights, Patti and I bouncing like maniacs, playacting at rock stardom. Then imagine Paul, nylon and kilt, classmates staring up at him in awe, parents in the back in disbelief. Watch him wail away at that guitar, reach way down inside himself to a place he hadn't ever shown anyone. Maybe you won't be able to see it, to understand his struggle with life, with the simple burden of being alive, with confusion and anger and hunger for something, anything, better. Maybe I didn't see it either. Maybe all I saw were three friends making noise.

"Top five bands that you discovered since high school that you can't live without. Go."

Behind Patti, Seattle's Puget Sound sparkles in the remarkable afternoon sunshine. I glance at her sideways.

"Bands or individual artists?" I ask. "Am I not allowed to have listened to any of them in high school, but they were around back then?"

She shoves me. "Just list, bitchface, don't overthink."

I overthink everything related to music. Just like Paul. It's been two-and-a-half years now since he died, and it's the first time I've seen Patti since we stood outside Paul's house last Christmas.

"Fuck it," she says, shifting in her seat and pulling her legs up. "I'll go."

We flew into Seattle separately, rented a car, and are driving to Portland before routing back to the middle of Washington state for a three-day music festival called Sasquatch.

"Smiths, Silver Jews, Modest Mouse . . ."

"Modest Mouse?" I ask.

"Oh yeah. My roommates in LA listen to them constantly. I love that band."

Before moving to Los Angeles, Patti lived in Portland, Oregon, and before that, she lived in Nashville, Tennessee. That's where Paul and Patti moved after college, where he proposed, where they began their life together. We're driving to Portland today to retrieve some personal items she left at a friend's house.

"Bonnie 'Prince' Billy and . . . Arcade Fire."

"Obviously. You know, after Paul's funeral—"

Patti puts a hand on my leg. "I don't wanna talk about that right now."

I clam up. All I want to talk about is Paul.

After his funeral, I came back to Chicago in a cloud. I was waiting tables at a place I hated amidst a series of jobs I hated, floating through a haze, unsure of what I was doing with my life, or even what I wanted to be doing. In fact, the haze of uncertainty had lasted since I graduated college, and I'm starting to think the haze is a never-ending restlessness that will be my life forever.

"Pull in here," Patti instructs, and I park in the driveway of a one-story house in Portland. There's a man standing on the porch out front. He's a little bit older than us, wearing a faded T-shirt and jeans, covered in sweat and dirt.

"Hiya, Patti," he says as we get out of the car, opening his arms for a hug. Patti introduces me, and we exchange pleasantries, talk about our journey to Sasquatch, bands we're excited to see, etc.

"Well, all your stuff is back where you left it," he says with a jerk of his thumb. "It's my workstation now, so it's pretty dusty down there. I haven't had a chance to clean up."

We go into the basement, bare but for a couple of benches and tools. Every inch is covered in sawdust.

"He makes furniture," Patti explains. She leads me to a small closet in the corner of the room. The door is half-open, and Patti wrenches it all the way.

"Oh my god," she says.

The stereo equipment and books and duffle bags of clothes and stacks upon stacks of records that we are meant to pack up and ship to Los Angeles, all of it, packed in a rush and thrown here quickly, sticking out of crates with no top, are covered in a fine layer of sawdust.

"Shit," Patti says, hugging herself.

"If we clear this area," I say, looking around for a broom, "I can take out the records one by one and dust them off."

"Those are Paul's records," she says, and I stop.

"Hey, Nick," Paul would say, glancing up from his guitar, "when you die, can I have your record collection?"

I'd chuckle. I owned CDs. "'Course, Paul. Can I have yours?" His collection—of actual records—tripled the size of mine.

"Oh hell no," Paul would reply. "I'm gonna be buried with mine."

But now, here they are. I don't know how or why Patti trekked them across the country with her, and she doesn't say. She kneels down and examines the vinyl carefully, pulling out a Beach Boys album to investigate the damage. I wonder what is constantly roiling inside her, what darkness sits on her chest, attacks her at night, wakes her screaming from nightmares. But I can't ask her. Not now.

"I can't deal with this," she says. "Let's just take my clothes and get out of here."

We pack what we can carry in one load, Patti apologizing to her friend, whose name I don't recall and will never see again. We leave behind the music Paul spent a lifetime collecting, relics of a dead man, never to surface or spin again.

We remain silent. We don't speak as Patti drives east out of Portland, into the high desert, vast and open. We follow the Columbia River, curving north through Washington, passing Yakima to the Sasquatch campgrounds. In the morning, we awake to a stunning view: miles of brown hills stretching into the distance, eons of blue sky all around us. The amphitheater rests at the bottom of a gorge, a remote and beautiful expanse. For three days, we fly from stage to stage, making friends with Canadians, drinking a lot, and waking up early with the sunshine. We do not talk. Not really. Not the kind of heart-to-heart that we regularly shared in high school. Not even the one we shared six months ago.

We're too close here, sharing a tent, going everywhere together. Maybe we both know, despite the miles of space and thousands of people, there's nowhere for us to go if one of us says the wrong thing. I'm constantly ready to delve into the past, learn more secrets, but she isn't. I don't know why I thought three days in the middle of nowhere would return us someplace that will never be the same.

After the festival closes, we drive back to Seattle. It's late at night, and I have to fight to stay awake while Patti dozes next to me. At one point, she stirs and reaches to turn down the music.

"He got really sick," she blurts out.

"Huh?" I ask.

"Paul," she says. "He got really sick. He wasn't the person we remember. One time, he went after me with a machete, cornered me in the kitchen. Our neighbor broke down the door and tackled him."

"Jesus. Patti, that's . . ."

"I know," she says.

I wonder if we're both thinking the same thing, that if Paul got violent with Patti, then something major had snapped inside him, some inner darkness had been released. And even though I know I shouldn't ask the question that everyone asks, the question that can't be answered, I do.

"What happened to him?"

Patti stifles a sob but keeps going. "I don't know. Maybe it was always buried inside him and finally burst. Maybe there was a trigger that I'll never know about. Our last Christmas was the best day we ever spent together. Two days later, he was gone."

My hands grip the steering wheel tight. Patti and I will never be returned to before, to high school, the talent show, after schools in the backyard, all the mundane moments of our friendship. We trudge through the After, picking up the pieces that Paul shattered so that we can somehow move forward. It won't fill either of us with a tingling, overwhelming fullness. But I know that we will cling to each other and never let go.

I say nothing and drive through the darkness towards morning.

Two weeks before we left for college, Patti and I threw a party at her house while her parents were out of town. We invited everyone from high school and made a drink called Hop, Skip, and Go Naked: vodka, beer, and lemonade concentrate.

"You know how you wanna get laid tonight?" Patti asked, bounding out the screen door to find me smoking alone on the back porch.

"Um, yes," I said, taking the drink Patti offered. I was desperate to lose my virginity before college. I was such a cliché.

Patti flicked her eyes to the kitchen, where a pretty girl in all black ladled some hooch into her cup, careful not to spill it on the floor.

"You're not serious," I said. "Megan?"

Patti set her cup down and placed her hands on my shoulders. "Nick, Paul dumped her. You go to college in two weeks. It's a party. Loosen up."

Two weeks before, Patti and Paul and I had sat on the same floor in Patti's kitchen while I cried about girls, like always. I didn't date much in high school; I was awkward and repressed and never knew what to say. We were doing what we always did: if one person is down, the other two helped them stand up.

"What if I never get anyone to like me, ever?" I asked.

Patti chuckled. "You will. Someday soon, what Paul and I are saying will all make sense." Patti had had sex with Matthew, her first love, whom she started dating around the time she started hanging out with us.

"And if it doesn't?" I asked.

Patti looked to Paulie like, "You gonna help me out here?" Paul looked bored, lying sideways on the linoleum floor, staring up at the ceiling. Maybe he was embarrassed by my neediness. I hadn't seen him that much lately. We'd acted in a play that summer but hardly spoken to each other. Once, after rehearsal, I asked him to walk with me to my car. On a suburban side street, the streetlamp barely illuminating our faces, I asked him if we were doing okay, if our friendship was okay. He shrugged, barely suppressing a scoff. He looked off into the distance. "Yeah, man," was all he said.

When Patti looked at him, he shrugged and said, "We can at least help you get laid." He had lost it back when we were fourteen, when I dreamed of just kissing girls, and slept with every girl he had dated after, including a pretty sophomore named Megan, who—two weeks later—was suddenly not his girlfriend and standing right in front of me.

"Killer party," she said. "You have a cigarette?"

I fished in my pockets for my pack and gave one to her.

"Thanks," she said, smiling up at me. She was gorgeous, petite with large black eyes, smart as hell, and even though she was a few years younger, she was way more self-assured than I was.

"Wanna go sit on the swing set?" she asked. Behind her, Patti nodded her head vigorously.

"Yeah," I said, butterflies creeping into my belly. Pretty girls like Megan never wanted to go sit on swing sets in dark corners of backyards with me—they wanted to do that with Paul. But I was just drunk enough not to think about any of that, about Paul or the party or leaving for college and never coming back.

We sat down, and Megan kissed me. A bomb went off in my stomach. She placed her hand on the inside of my thigh. She whispered in my ear, "Let's go upstairs." We waded through the party hand in hand, past drunk friends and spilled booze, ignoring the turned heads. As we got to the front of the house, where the main door met the stairwell, Paul entered the party with his new girlfriend, a blonde in heels. We nearly collided with them and exchanged a glance, he and I, quick and furtive.

Megan pulled me up to the second floor. We found an open bedroom, Patti's parents' room. We kissed some more, her lips on my neck, tongue in my ear; her hands moved over my belt, undid each loop, unbuttoned my pants, and took them off. "Remove your shirt," she commanded, and I did. She pushed me down on the bed and climbed on top. We jostled back and forth, my hands on her waist, steadying myself, moving to a dance I didn't yet know, a rhythm that felt so goddamn-holy-cow good. And then?

It was over. That was it? That's what I had cried about?

A few days later, Paul called me at home.

"Well," Paul said. "I guess congratulations are in order."

"Uh, thanks," I said.

Paul was silent. The phone shook in my hands.

"So, Nick, I think that's pretty much it for us. You know; don't call. Or anything. Goodbye."

The next time I saw Paul would be at Patti's twenty-first birthday party.

The time after that, he was dead.

"Nick, are you sitting down?"

"Ashley? Hi?" I straddled a fire hydrant and pulled my scarf tight. Ashley was a friend of ours from high school, a senior when we were juniors, and Patti's roommate for a year in college. I'd not spoken to her in three years. "What's going on?"

It was my second winter in Chicago, a year and a half out of theatre school, and I waited tables at a fine-dining restaurant in River North. The night was slow, calm before the New Year's Eve storm, and I looked forward to catching a cab home for an early night's sleep.

Ashley took a deep breath.

"Paul Myers killed himself."

"Oh my god." A cab pulled up, but I waved it off.

"Patti asked me to call you," she said.

"I haven't seen them in three years." Or spoken or emailed or texted.

"Nick. She found him."

I went silent. Numbness crept over me.

"The funeral is Monday. You should come home."

The last time I saw them, it was Patti's twenty-first birthday party in East Lansing. I made the trek from Ohio to celebrate. This was a big deal; I rarely left my university bubble with my new friends and killer parties. But it was Patti. Not being there was out of the question.

The party was at her off-campus apartment, a long, narrow building with a shared balcony. The cold blistered our faces as we huddled outside smoking, the warmth inside fogging our glasses. People came and went, Patti's new friends in her new life. I played drinking games, downed beer, smoked pot. Patti whirled around the tiny pad, hugging people without stopping to really speak to them. Paul was there, but I didn't talk to him. He had invited me to his twenty-first birthday party the previous summer, but after devastating me, hurting me worse than anyone in my life up to that point had, I wanted nothing to do with him.

Nicholas Ward

Later, after most of the guests had departed, I had a cigarette on the balcony, wanting everyone to leave so I could crash on the couch and go home. To Ohio.

The door opened, and Patti threw her arms around me, her cheek pressed against my back.

"Thank you for coming," she whispered. "I'm sorry we didn't really talk."

She leaned next to me over the ledge. She had replaced her black party dress with pj's and a peacoat, hair poking out under a Montreal Canadiens hat.

"So, those are my friends," she said.

"They seem nice."

"They are," she said. "I like to be surrounded by people I love."

The door creaked open.

"I have something to tell you," Patti started, while Paul joined her on the other side.

"Actually," Paul took her hand, sliding his fingers into hers, "we have something to tell you."

I remember flicking my cigarette onto the concrete and stubbing it out with my boot.

I remember taking a final swig of my beer and heaving the bottle into the parking lot, where it shattered on the pavement.

I remember laughing. A snotty sneer, right in their faces.

"Um . . ." It was Patti. "Not exactly the reaction we were looking for?"

"Seriously?" I asked them.

Paul slipped his arm around her waist. "I've been in love with her for years, man."

"Okay," I backed away from them, arms outward. "I should just go."

"No!" Patti said. "We were hoping you'd stay and talk. We want to tell you everything."

"You can't just drop that bomb on me and expect me to react like everything is A-OK."

You might think that I was in love with one, or both, of them.

But in my mind, Patti had a choice to make between romance and friendship, between Paul and Nick. I know now that she didn't choose Paul over me; she tried to choose both of us, and I couldn't see it.

"You couldn't have told me this was going on?" I asked. "I'm like, five hours away. It's not like I went anywhere far."

"Life happens," Patti said. "I don't have time to just hop on the phone and make sure you're doing okay."

The next thing I said, I will regret forever.

"You would if you were my real friend."

No one spoke for a long time. Patti leaned into Paul's chest.

"Nick, I think you should leave," Paul said.

Tears streamed down my cheeks. I gathered my belongings and spent the night in my car, feeling left out again of that once beautiful circle and empty. When the sun came up and I had sobered up, I drove back to school.

I was early to Paul's wake. A couple of cars dotted the parking lot of the Thayer-Rock Funeral Home. I took a deep breath, my hand on the door. I opened it.

She was on me immediately, a wave of wild, curly red hair smothering me in a hug.

For all I know, our embrace overtook the small foyer, grief-stricken friends and relatives forced to scoot around us as they entered and exited. I didn't give a shit. It felt good to cry into her again. It felt like home.

"What the fuck?" I blurted.

She started laughing. "I know, right?" Music played faintly in the distance, a new song I really liked by the Yeah Yeah Yeahs.

She put her arms on my shoulders, and we looked each other square in the eyes.

"Let's go see Paul," she said.

She led me to the casket, past an assembled collage of photos and a laptop playing music. He looked unreal lying there. He'd hanged himself, gruesomely slumped forward on his bathroom toilet, belt tied to the window behind him. It took force and determination for him to die. To make him look presentable to us, they'd shaved off most of his beard, leaving only a mustache that was so not Paul.

Standing there felt like years, like we were making up for lost time, communicating in a language only we could understand. I didn't know then that Paul's death would give my life meaning, that, since he died, I've come to anticipate the funeral around every corner, tried to fill each moment of each day with a love that is buried deep in my stomach, to share that secret and vulnerable part of myself.

Patti interlocked her fingers with mine.

"What's with the mustache?" I asked.

She grinned. "That's what I said. I don't know why they just didn't shave that off too." Her eyes were puffy from crying, but she was smiling, her gaze fixed on Paul. "I half expect him to jump up, do a little Paulie dance, rip off that stupid mustache and shout 'Just kidding!'"

We laughed despite ourselves. We needed to.

"When I found him . . ." she trailed off. That story could wait. "But he looks peaceful now."

We stood silent, holding hands. When we exhaled, it was in perfect unison.

"I don't know how this is possible," I say, fishing out the last Parliament Light for Patti while she passes me the bottle of cheap chardonnay, "but you always look the same to me, in my memory or right now. Different hairstyles or colors, new tattoos, glasses, contacts, crying, smiling, snow, summer, you're always eighteen years old to me. We could be anywhere in the world, at any time."

"But we're not," she says, with a nod to the old farmhouse, gussied up with a new addition to the back so it looks familiar yet unrecognizable in the same breath.

"I want to tell him things," I say.

"Like what?" she asks.

"Little things," I say. "That he'd probably like Arcade Fire a lot."

Patti smiles. "Yeah, he would."

And you'd probably like LCD Soundsystem too, Paul, and The XX and Janelle Monae.

And I wish you could read what I wrote about you. I wish I could tell you that you visited me in my dreams, talked to me like you were alive, told me everything was going to be okay. I wish you didn't die and that the three of us—you, me, and Patti—could sit in your backyard as adults and listen to you play music. I'd smoke cigarettes, even though I haven't had one in a long time, and maybe your daughter would sit on Patti's lap, and your mom would cook platters of vegetables and gossip with my mom, and our dads would talk awkwardly while they grilled meat, and we could all just be together, one big family.

I rock on my feet, and the snow crunches; the wine twists in my guts. Patti passes our final cigarette, and I finish it quickly, stubbing it out on the ground. It's time to go soon, me back to Chicago, Patti to LA where she moved after Portland, after Nashville, after Michigan.

We hug, deep and full—like that night at the funeral home. She touches my face with her hands. "A month before he died, Paul told me that he missed you terribly, that he thought about you a lot. He felt bad about how things had ended. He wanted you back in his life."

"Really?" I ask.

Her gloves grab the lapels of my coat. "He loved you, Nick. And this," Patti gestures to the house, but I knew what she meant, "this is how he brought us back together."

I don't know what to say. I am overwhelmed and overjoyed and tired and full.

"I'll see you soon," I whisper.

"Yes," Patti says. "Soon."

We Travel the City

Once we decided to move in together, all Karen and I could talk about was where we wanted to live.

"I don't think I can stay in Roscoe much longer," Karen said. Located on Chicago's North Side, Roscoe Village is all tree-lined streets, independent boutiques, and neighborhood taverns.

"Why not?" I asked. We were having breakfast at John's Place, a bright and casual family spot. Karen set down her coffee mug, nudged aside the almost empty plates in front of her, and reached across the table. She focused her eyes on mine.

"I just don't think this is a place for me," she said.

Karen is biracial, with a white mother from Wisconsin and a Black father from Cincinnati.

"I thought we were all post-racial now," I said.

Karen shot me a don't-be-stupid look. Before we started dating, I subscribed—if I thought about it at all—to non-racist liberalism. Back then, if I'm being honest, I took a pull from the post-racial elixir. If a biracial man could be elected president, maybe transcending race was possible. But I learned pretty quickly how that ideology was insufficient and maybe a little dangerous. I shouldn't have had to date a Black woman to unlearn harmful ideas about race. But dating Karen set me on a path towards understanding the social and political project of whiteness for the first time. It's a lengthy process.

A mid-thirties white couple with a baby stroller was seated next to us, the restaurant filling up after church. Out of the corner of my eye, I watched the man give us a quick once-over. It was subtle, just a glance from me to her, but Karen saw it too. That happened all the time, from white ladies who lunch to the tattooed yuppies like the ones seated next to us.

Karen raised an eyebrow in my direction. I gave a shrug of assent.

"Can we get outta here?" Karen asked, checking her wristwatch. "We need to hustle up." We were due at Matt and Stefanie's new home, a long journey to the far South Side, for a holiday weekend "staycation."

I nodded. "Swing by your place, then mine, then go?"

Karen and I had met at the first rehearsal of a play. She waltzed into the theatre, threw her bag down, and unraveled layer upon layer of winter clothing. Warmth radiated outward from her, and I stood entranced a few rows away. I swear I could hear angels singing, birds cooing softly, bells ringing. At the final cast party two months later, afraid I'd never see her again, I told her she was beautiful and asked her out.

I was coming off a string of brief but tumultuous relationships: a whispered goodbye over the phone with Amelia, a public breakup at a coffee shop with Leah, a shouting match outside in the cold with Em. With each breakup, I cast about further:

working too hard, drinking in too many bars, trying to locate whatever magic I thought I could discover in another person.

We fell into a life together. For eighteen months, we'd lived two blocks from each other off Addison, a mile west of Wrigley Field. It was good for our relationship. We spent equal time at each other's apartments, and while we quarreled about other things, we never argued about being too far away from home. We enjoyed that neighborhood together: the bar on the corner with the ever-rotating taps, the restaurant where they knew us by sight, if not by name, the famous bakery on Lincoln Avenue where we went Sunday mornings and read the paper like two adults growing old together. But now that we were taking the next step, we had to really think about where we wanted to settle. I liked Roscoe Village. I was comfortable there. It was well-positioned for me needing to get around the city without a car. But also, the neighborhood was super white.

Back then, I assumed that our biracial coupling alone wasn't drawing attention. Karen was flat-out gorgeous; she walked into a room and changed the quality of the air. Strangers approached her on the street to tell her she looked like Rihanna; men followed her through aisles in Target to say hello. At the time, I never saw the attention the world bestowed on her as racialized. She was just pretty.

We paid and left the restaurant, walking arm in arm on that sunny Sunday, streets teeming with strollers and dogs.

It would be almost another year before we made the move; we both liked our apartments, our roommates, had leases we didn't feel like we could break. Even still, we couldn't help ourselves.

"I like Andersonville," Karen said, referring to a community by the lake and north a few miles. Historically Swedish, still majority white, it was bordered by Black and Asian neighborhoods to the east and far more diverse than Roscoe.

"It's so far away," I said. "What about Logan Square?"

That earned me a playful elbow in the ribs. Karen found

Logan insufferable, mostly due to the influx of hipsters like her friend Julian, who claimed that Logan Square was "where the real Chicago lived."

"Hello!" Matt shouted as we walked up, standing with Stefanie on the wide cement porch of their two-story, red-brick bungalow. They'd recently purchased the home at 95th and Leavitt in Beverly, twenty miles away from Roscoe Village—way farther south in Chicago than I'd ever been.

"So," Stefanie said in her flat Midwestern accent, "I hear you're thinking of moving in together. Where are you looking?"

We'd settled in, side by side, on the porch swing, beers thrust into our palms, our friends beaming from ear to ear.

"Andersonville," Karen said. "Logan Square," I said at the same time, needling her.

"I love Logan Square," Stefanie said. They'd just moved from there.

"Me too," said Matt. "It's where real people live."

Karen gave me an are-you-shitting-me look. I shrugged my shoulders and smiled.

My friends couldn't wait to show us their home: their enormous bedroom, basement wine cellar, enclosed back porch, backyard with a hammock where the dogs ran around freely.

"You ever think about wanting all this?" I asked Karen. We were in the first-floor guest room, changing into clothes to go out.

"What?" Karen asked. "Marriage, house, comfort, impending children, stable income? Of course." Lingering between us was the unspoken question of whether or not we wanted that life with each other. I wasn't sure if I wanted that life at all. I'm still not. And once we answered that question, our life together wouldn't last much longer. "But I'm not moving down here to get it." Though in the same city, on tree-lined streets just like ours, Beverly felt like a radically different universe.

"Why'd they move down here?" she continued.

"It's a good place to live," I said. "Stef's family is close." Her sprawling Lithuanian community lived in Evergreen Park, a suburb a half-mile west.

"What about Matt? What does he get?"

I didn't know. Moving to Beverly put him far away from me and his other friends. His family lived in Cleveland. The shift had upended his social circle, but he did seem to genuinely enjoy living there.

"Baby, that's what you're gonna wear?" Karen asked.

I looked at my white tank top. "I thought we were casual today."

She peered at me. "Maybe too casual." She was wearing a multi-colored sundress, black hair pulled back, and huge sunglasses. She looked radiant.

I grabbed a white, collared shirt to throw over it.

"Is this what it means to get older?" I asked.

"You talking about the clothes or the house?"

"Both?"

The bar was at 106th and Western, no-man's-land as far as I was concerned, and packed.

"I didn't know it was gonna be so crowded," Matt said. We stood abreast outside the steel door of the bar, looking at the back patio.

"It's Labor Day, Matt," Stefanie said. "Of course it's crowded."

He looked to Karen and me. "Get drinks and find a seat?"

"Why not," Karen said. "I didn't walk all this way for nothing."

Karen had pouted about going; we could visit a bar any time on the North Side and didn't this hammock look relaxing? But Matt insisted, wanting to show off his new neighborhood. He led us on a forty-five-minute stroll through Beverly, past the rows of flourishing homes and carefully manicured lawns. The walk through the heart of the neighborhood was idyllic: kids playing on the streets, the trees a canopy above our heads. Beverly is both middle-class and integrated, one of the few Chicago neighborhoods where people of different races live next to one another. Never mind the cul-de-sacs along 95th street that prevent unwanted traffic from entering the community. Nothing to see there.

Matt smiled the whole way, happy to play the flaneur with his friends. I realized how comfortable he was already, how the city, with its bustle and noise, held no allure for him like it did for Karen and me, how their move wasn't solely about Stefanie and her family.

"Are we almost there?" Karen asked, annoyed.

"Just a bit," Stef told her. "We have to go to the other side of Western. Beverly is dry."

"It's been that way forever," Matt said.

"Doesn't mean it should stay that way," Karen said.

If I'd known then that crossing the street meant entering Mount Greenwood, that Mount Greenwood was a breeding ground for white supremacy, that residents would openly celebrate the police shooting of a young Black man many years later, I'm not sure what I would have done. I was completely clueless. And if Karen herself knew, she didn't say anything. We just wanted to get a beer, after all.

"Everybody is looking at us," Karen said. She hooked an arm through my elbow.

The bar was beautiful, a multi-tiered deck with a sturdy oak in the center. A local radio station, Q-something-something, was broadcasting live in the corner by a sign advertising a White Sox promo event. The people—white, all of them— lounged at long wood tables guzzling Old Style by the pitcher. They wore Sox jerseys and hats, had unshaved stubble on their faces, beer guts sticking out with pride. We were wearing collared shirts and sundresses. We stuck out.

Nicholas Ward

Karen leaned over to me. "Please tell me this isn't going to be like that bar in Logan Square," she said.

"Which one?" I asked.

"Tell me you didn't forget."

A few months before, at the tail end of winter, Karen and I tried to go to this new cocktail bar called The Whistler. While we waited for the line to subside, not wanting to stand outside in the cold, we took respite in the dive bar across the street, Helen's Two-Way Lounge.

The Two-Way was loud and crowded, the warmth from the bodies fogging my glasses. The bar straddled the corner of a six-way intersection, with entrance doors on opposite sides. Karen and I headed for a pair of seats at an open table. There were some people standing near them but no empty glasses on the tabletop or coats on the stools.

"Actually, these seats are taken," a white guy in flannel and skinny jeans said.

"Oh," we said. "Sorry."

Karen and I shared a look and then took in our surroundings. The half of the bar we entered, populated by shoulder-high tables and a new electronic jukebox, was filled entirely with mid-twenties white people in skinny jeans, cute dresses, beards, and funky hair. We turned our attention to the back half of the bar, where a group of people clustered around a game of pool. We saw Latinx people, a few Black folks, and some white people too.

We found a spot to stand in the middle. We ordered two cheap beers and drank them, mostly silent.

A small white guy came up to us. I couldn't tell which side he'd come from.

"What's up?" he said

"Not much," I said.

He swayed a little, uneasy on his feet, eyes glassy. Behind

him, people waited in line for the bathroom and put quarters down on the pool table.

"How do you feel about Obama?!" he shouted.

Technically, I suppose, he could've been asking both of us, but the blotto stare in Karen's direction let us know exactly who he was barking at.

Karen turned to me sharply. "I don't care where, but we gotta go."

The four of us found a table in back, on the raised level, where we could look out at the crowd.

"Cheers," Stef said. "So great to have you both down to our neck of the woods."

Behind Stef, a woman leaned over to the man next to her and looked in Karen's direction. I gripped her hand under the table. Matt said something I couldn't hear to his wife, and she patted his knee with a laugh.

We sat sipping our beers.

Karen's knee bounced in agitation.

Matt and Stefanie spoke with each other, small talk about the house.

I scanned the crowd, my head swiveling, as the laughter and radio broadcast coalesced into white noise, faceless bodies enjoying their well-earned time off.

"See, no one's gonna say anything," I said to Karen.

Matt heard me and gave me a quizzical look.

"Can I tell him?" I asked Karen.

"Go ahead," she said, with a wave of her hand outward.

I told the story of the encounter at the Two-Way. I told it like a joke with a punchline. I figured a few months had dulled the sting of the experience.

"That's just so messed up," I said, gesturing to Karen, "that someone could look at you and just peg you like that." She took a sip of beer and nodded to me in terse silence.

Nicholas Ward

"When we first moved to Chicago," Matt said, thinking he was being helpful, "to Logan Square, people would come up to me on the street and ask me questions in Spanish, thinking I was Mexican. You remember that, dude?"

"Matt," Karen snapped, "you promised me burgers."

"They're waiting for us at home, ready for the grill. By the time we drink more, we'll be ready to eat."

We walked back up Western Avenue, Karen and I in front, Matt and Stef twenty feet behind. The return journey was through an ugly part of Chicago, all car dealerships and fast-food restaurants and corporate chain stores. I'm not sure why we strayed from the idyllic streets we took to the bar; maybe there was nothing left for Matt and Stefanie to show us.

"You don't get it," she said. "Even if no one says anything, it still hurts. These looks are every second of my life."

I didn't say anything. I didn't know if I would ever have the courage to support her in the ways that she needed. But I knew I had a lot more to understand. I looked at all these businesses we were passing on the street, the same in every neighborhood, whether corporate or independent, groovy craft cocktail spots or corner bars, grocery stores or bakeries or CVS pharmacies, and I thought about all these spaces, how I could enter them anonymously and never have to worry.

I snuck my fingers into her palm, clasping her hand with mine. "You don't wanna live down here, do you?" I asked.

She laughed. "Never ever, ever."

"Jokes," I said. "We can live wherever you want."

She eased an arm around my waist. I slung mine over her shoulder. We walked like that the rest of the way, cars humming past us on that nondescript stretch of the city.

Life as a Smoker

1981

He is born, the child of two public school teachers who are both nonsmokers.

'90s

He is taught the dangers of smoking; cigarettes are the "gateway" to pot and alcohol and, eventually, crack cocaine. Even in the suburbs, everyone is obsessed by the idea of crack: fearful of its powers, determined to keep their children safe. At his mostly white public schools, he is warned of nicotine's addictive properties, shown photos of black lungs. One winter, on a family drive to visit his grandparents in Ohio, he develops a coughing fit that lasts the entire five hours. Shortly thereafter, he is diagnosed with asthma. Good, his parents think; at least he'll never smoke.

1997

At sixteen, he smokes his first cigarette in the park behind Ryan's house, under the jungle gym. They spend many afternoons that summer smoking just two cigarettes each, one after the other. If someone comes along, a kid with parents, they stub them out casually in the gravel.

They're thrilled. Smoking is forbidden but easy. For years, whole summers revolve around bumbling through their suburban town, smoking. No one's parents (least of all Ryan's) expect them to stay near the house or tell anyone where they're going. They can slip away to the park, sneak back into the house covertly, and wash their hands of the stench.

Ryan works at Subway, alongside an older girl, a senior, who buys them packs. She takes the $2.50 they scrounge together to Tweeny's, a party store across the way, for a pack of Marlboro Lights. In the beginning, a pack might last ten days or two weeks.

It's not that bad, he tells himself. He'll never get addicted.

1998

Cigarettes are surprisingly available. Either his thirty-two-year-old boss at the Pasta Stop supplies them or he borrows his dad's Ford Escort for a run to the Shell gas station at 9 Mile and Farmington Road. They sell to minors when no one else is watching.

On prom night, he finds himself hanging out at the house of his old friend, Paul Myers, with whom he'd once been closely acquainted. While their dates watch television in Paul's house— his parents asleep or out of town—the two boys smoke in the backyard, looking out over the rows of vegetables, the old barn, the long-defunct chicken coop. They talk about music and movies, about their psychology class, about how they don't really understand high school or the people in it. They promise to hang out more often.

His habit—like his reunited friendship with Paul—really takes flight.

He starts working at his first proper restaurant, Bill Knapp's. The restaurant provides a smoking section off the main dining room and a back break station where he sits with his coworkers, smoking cigarettes, munching on fries, drinking coffee at all hours. When his parents question the smell, he lies easily, tells them he worked in Smoking Section for the night. "You need to ask them not to schedule you there," they say. "It's not good for your asthma."

"It's not that bad," he replies, wondering if they know the truth. His manager shows him her adolescent trick, to rub his hands with lemons before he leaves. This way, only his clothes reek of the restaurant—smoke and grease and the bits of bean soup that splatter onto his blue shirt—but he will remain fresh as a daisy.

1999

Paul turns eighteen two months before he does, and the days of fretting over their acquisition are in the rearview mirror. They smoke Parliament Lights, P-Funks, peppered increasingly with marijuana, inside Paul's family barn or at the end of his yard, far away from the house. Or they smoke in his parents' garage, stubbing them out in the oil stains dripping from the cars, leaving the door open for twenty minutes to air it out properly, wrapping them in Kleenex before stuffing them in the white trash can. When his father inquires as to why his garbage smells like smoke, he blames it on Paul, which is shitty.

In the winter, on nights when he can't sleep, he smokes on the side of his parents' house, near where his mom plants flowers in the spring. He shuffles onto a small patch of pavement where firewood is stacked for the long, cold months ahead. He thinks about the times when firewood was necessary to heat an entire family home, not merely an affectation of the middle-class. He dreams about leaving that place. All throughout that winter, he tosses his smokes into the snow on the neighbor's side. In the spring, when the snow thaws, he discovers the resiliency of cigarette butts—he'll have to find another place to dispose of them.

2000

He gets caught.

It's after school—that window between 2:45 p.m. and 4:30 p.m. when he's home alone, free to sing and masturbate and smoke, all of which he does with voracity. One day, at ten past three, he opens the door from the kitchen to the garage to find his mother pulling her car in.

"Why is the garage door open?" she asks.

"What are you doing home?"

"I had an early doctor's appointment, I told you that. Why does it smell like smoke?"

"..."

"Nick."

He doesn't stop. His mother smoked in college, and he hopes she'll understand. She doesn't tell his father; she tries her best to hide her son's habits from her husband, who never tried cigarettes or marijuana a day in his life, who "doesn't understand why smart people would start smoking."

In college, later that year, he meets his best friends Will, Matt, and Rance smoking on the steps of his dorm. Matt and Rance are buddies from high school, and they offer to host the smokers in their room during the winter or when they're too drunk or lazy to go outside. Rance is obsessed with cigarettes—always playing with the packs, twirling them through his fingers, but never actually smoking them. He doesn't understand how Rance puts up with smoking, in their freshman and sophomore dorm rooms, or in Barcelona, where he moves after school and still lives. The man has been surrounded by smoking for decades. How doesn't it bother him?

Will is a fellow theatre major, and all the theatre kids smoke because they're dramatic and ridiculous and young; at parties, they compose indulgent, digressive, alcohol-infused, and pot-laced odes to cigarettes, to college, to life. He thinks they're the most fun and exciting group of people he's ever met.

He claims he's not addicted.

"When did you start smoking?" his new friend, Aaron, asks.

"Sixteen."

"How old are you now?"

"Nineteen."

"You're addicted."

2001

Second semester, he develops a morning ritual with Jeff, a guy from his dorm. It seems that they're the only two guys on their all-male floor who wake up a few hours before their 9 a.m. classes to eat and enjoy the morning. They have breakfast together and then retire to Jeff's room, where they gaze onto the courtyard, over the soft dew of the late-winter morning, watching the students crisscrossing on their way to and from class. Over two cigarettes each, they talk about their own classes, their lives, books they're reading, before shoving off for the day. They never become close, though perhaps they share something more intimate in those moments that they won't ever recapture on campus: a silence with someone who understands them.

2002

Sophomore year. Two days a week, he has 8 a.m. classes. He rises at six, smokes a cigarette, eats breakfast, another cigarette, quick shower, two more smokes on the way to class. He continues like this throughout the day; it's not uncommon to consume thirty cigarettes—a pack and a half—over the course of a single day. One Thursday begins at 6 a.m. and ends after a night of drinking at four in the morning, and over the course of the day, he smokes three packs of cigarettes.

His roommates, Will and Matt and John (who isn't their roommate but who's just always around) spend the second half of the year taping their empty packs against the wall outside his and Matt's room, all the Parliaments and Camels and Marlboro Lights and Djarums and the occasional Reds and Winstons and Lucky Strikes and Full Flavors that they've consumed over four months, a living, wheezing collage in salute of smoking.

Of course, he thinks he looks cooler smoking than not smoking. He grew up on *Goodfellas* and *Pulp Fiction* and *The Man Who Wasn't There*, films that make their characters look edgier, hipper, and harder with cigarettes in their mouths. He fashions himself an iconoclast, rebelling against proper society, smoking in defiance of a world that is slowly learning to disdain the habit. He's unaware that he's actually pumping all of his excess income into one of the biggest corporations our culture has ever known, into a legacy laced with blood.

2002 - 2003

He lives alone for the first time in his life. He thinks living by himself will cure whatever it is that ails him. He doesn't investigate what that might be, why he finds himself sad and miserable for stretches at a time, why he worries, at twenty-one, that he's undeserving of love and affection. It's the worst and the loneliest year of his life. Without a cell phone, he finds meeting up with friends difficult; his apartment is always cold; he doesn't yet know how to cook; he fails to study with any real diligence, spending most of his waking hours outside of class watching sports and smoking and drinking. Often, he will sit in his bathtub in tepid water and smoke, flicking ashes into the sink. Sometimes he takes a shit and does the same thing.

There are many happy memories from this year: watching *Cruel Intentions 2* with Betsy and drinking Boone's Farm and eating Häagen-Dazs and throwing parties that got way out of hand and even a few nights with girls that he liked, staying up late and talking.

In the fall of his senior year, he drives home to attend a Michigan State vs. Kentucky basketball game with his dad, held at the sparkling, new Ford Field in downtown Detroit. At halftime, when he exits onto the smokers' landing, he huddles in the cold with all the other smokers, men and women with sunken faces, hacking coughs, miserable expressions. He doesn't want to end up like that, a smoker in his forties or fifties still craving cigarettes, needing that buzz, that fix, something to do with his hands, smelling gross all the time. He will quit, he decides then and there. It's only a matter of time.

2004

He moves to Chicago with Will and Matt and Betsy and Stefanie, his smoking buddies. They all make an agreement to smoke less, to cut back. He gets down to five cigarettes a day—a necessity, since he's unable to find a job. He keeps borrowing money from his parents. He wasn't prepared for unemployment; he was certain he could wait tables. He doesn't want to spend that money on cigarettes, but by now both his parents know about his habit. He feels guilty and grateful to have parents who can, and will, support him. It won't be the first or last time in his life he'll need their help.

2005

He smokes his last cigarette sometime in September of that year. He returns home after a night of drinking wine with a girl he likes; there's one cigarette in his pack, and he smokes it delicately, reverently.

He actually lasts a few months. He shuffles cards, drinks lots of OJ, consumes less alcohol. And it works—more or less. He's miserable at times, but he's on a path towards a smoke-free life. Everyone else around him still lights up, which makes him itchy and irritable, but he knows what he has to do.

Then Paul dies and everything goes to shit. In the aftermath, with the guilt and hurt and shame and incomprehension, he picks up again. How could he not? Cigarettes have been the balm of his life; whenever he was stressed or bored or drunk or high, smoking was the immediate release, the inhale, the quiet moment, the only way he knew to shut the entire world out and focus on one small, simple task. Watching the smoke curl around his hands, feeling it in his lungs, releasing it out to the world, has been the only constant of his life. Did he really think he could drop it with the flick of a wrist?

2006 - 2008

He keeps trying to quit, but there's always something that pulls him back.

Drunken, dramatic, cold-weather breakup in front of Will and Betsy at his Roscoe Village apartment? Smoke.

Sweaty, boozy outdoor music festival in Union Park with sunlight and laughter and high-fives? Smoke.

Cast party in Ravenswood where he tells the woman in the play he thinks she's lovely and is profoundly embarrassed afterward? Smoke.

2008 - 2011

He dates the beautiful woman from the play. In the very beginning, she tells him she can't date a smoker, and he'd rather be with her than with cigarettes, so that is that.

Except . . . is every once in a while really so bad? When he's stoned with his roommate, Jay, in the empty upstairs apartment? Or after a few too many Three Floyds after work?

It's not quite that benign. He disgusts himself, tossing packs in the trash at night, only to liberate them the next morning. Once, he takes the pack of cigarettes all the way out to the dumpster in the alley. The next night, after a few pints at the Black Rock, he strongly considers diving into the dumpster, asking Jay to hold his feet. He doesn't do it but he's sickened even thinking about it.

Somewhere in there, he quits for a whole year. Not one cigarette for at least 365 days. He loves Karen; he wants to fully commit to her, but deep down in the places he doesn't wish to linger, he knows she isn't the one for him. It's not just the smoking. Not just their opposing religious viewpoints. Not just their fights over having children or his realization that her father disapproves of him or her headlong rush into running a business and focus on making money. It's everything.

Later, he won't remember when he picked up the habit again, but he does. And he begins to look forward to those moments when he can justify a cigarette, nights when she's out of town and won't be back 'til morning. Eventually, he starts smoking in her presence: when they go to France on vacation, at the New Year's Eve party they host, slipping out to contemplate the impending conversation the night he breaks up with her.

After he moves out, he doesn't care anymore. He buys packs, smokes on the balcony, spending afternoons after work watching the sun go down. He tells himself that he'll quit eventually, that he just has to want it, that it's not the right time yet, and only a little bit longer, all the lies he's been telling himself since he graduated college.

2012

The habit is still somehow enjoyable, but it's no longer worth it. He loves lounging in the lawn chairs in his backyard, his bare foot nestled in the space between Dina's thigh and the butt of the chair while they smoke and drink beers. He enjoys sharing a smoke after they fuck on Sundays, his friends watching baseball in the next room. But his throat always throbs the next day and his head spins—particularly if he's been drinking. Will, the person he'd been bumming from all year, finally quits smoking, and he'll grab a few here and there at parties, or even at work. But he's not going to buy a pack. Not after all this time.

He takes a twelve-day West Coast vacation by himself in September. In the past, this would've been an incubator for smoking: long stretches alone, occasional boredom, picturesque vistas, afternoon cocktails. But surprisingly, he doesn't smoke once.

October 5, 2012

He always imagined this moment tinged with grandeur, but when it happens, improbably and without warning, he doesn't even realize it's his last. It's only later, when he's reflecting on his whole smoking life, that the last cigarette achieves a sense of gravity.

At an after-work party, he bums a Camel Light from a coworker. He smokes it halfway, but the thrill is gone. It's not relaxing or tasty; it makes his throat dry and scratchy. He holds the butt between his thumb and middle finger, like he's done countless times over the previous fifteen years. The embers still burn. The ashes crackle and sway in the wind. He flicks it into the street.

The Lost Summer

Dina and I said "I love you" in the lobby of the Metro, plastered on whiskey. It was December. We held each other and kissed and said it and then kissed again. And again. And again. And then Dina went home with someone else.

We'd begun hooking up that spring. I'd been single for a year and was feeling like I was ready to get back into a relationship. At the bar down the street from the place we worked, Dina and I complained about our jobs over post-work cocktails, talked about art and our own careers. One night, in early March, we were joined by a few friends. After a series of rounds on an empty stomach, I leaned close and said, "Hey, I have some food at home I was going to make. Do you wanna have dinner with me?" She smiled, her rosy cheeks brightening. She looked so lovely that I couldn't believe I'd not asked her sooner. We got a ride back to my place in Roscoe Village from a guy in our group, and maybe he thought he was going to hook up with Dina because he followed us into my apartment, where we opened a bottle of wine. Eventually, he noticed us gravitating towards each other, no longer listening to a word he was saying, just smiling; he took off.

The next morning, she sat up in my bed. "Do you have 'Heroin'?" she asked.

I rubbed my eyes. "Um, what?" I replied.

"The song, boy, by The Velvet Underground."

"Oh," I said, reaching for my computer. "Of course."

"I like to listen to it while I'm getting ready."

She stood up, out of my bed, handing me my last half-full glass of wine from the night before. We cheers'd and got ready for work.

When I remember that spring, I think of the heat: seventy-five degrees in March, everybody walking around dazed from the thaw of a Chicago winter, wondering if it was real or not. Dina and I spent almost every night together, beers in my backyard that led to long nights, impromptu dates on outdoor patios. At first, we didn't want anyone to know that we were dating, so we'd arrive at parties a few minutes apart from each other and make eyes across the room, giggling that no one knew our secret.

The first time we talked about an open relationship was October. We'd spent all day celebrating her birthday: brunch followed by beers and movies at a friend's house in Palmer Square. It was while walking back to Dina's apartment through the fallen leaves of the boulevards, the world awash in amber, that we talked about what we wanted. It was so refreshing, to speak openly at the beginning of a relationship, to not automatically assume that our lives had to exist one way.

For years, I'd witnessed other men treat their girlfriends as nonentities. In college, my buddy Dave cheated on his future wife with such unabashed bravado that he kept long-term relationships with other women. I worked in restaurants where guys would arrange for their side pieces to meet them at work, even if their coworkers knew their wives or girlfriends. We had mutual friends who couldn't be in the same room together because of how much their affair had damaged their relationship. Monogamy was a sham. So why should we have to prescribe to that?

Dina and I had a very similar upbringing. Even though we were from opposite sides of the country, we both grew up in white middle-class homes. We spoke a lot about how our relationship pushed against the boundaries and expectations of our normative suburban upbringing. But if either of us knew that our lineage was formed by, and benefitted from, whiteness, we didn't say; we never talked about race and all that it entailed.

Our first real dust-up was the week before I moved into Dina's apartment. It was mid-April, a year or so after she'd first spent the night. "I'm freaking out," she said, "and I don't know if I'm ready for this."

We lay together on my couch. My entire life was in boxes— room rented, heart ready to create a home with her. "You're telling me now?" I demanded. "What am I supposed to do?"

"I don't know!" she said.

"Are you afraid we can't be open when we move in together?" I asked. The night before, we'd both gone on dates that ended as drunken hook-ups.

"Kinda," she said. "What if I need my space? What if you can't handle it?"

I cupped her face gently in my hands. "We get to define our relationship however we want. That's why we're open, right?"

She nodded. "If we break up, it's really gonna suck," she said.

"I know. But we'll never know how amazing it can be if we don't try."

I moved in a week later.

That summer was madness. It was the year of Daft Punk's return, the summer of light and bouncy beats, but it was also the summer that Chicago's gun violence hit national headlines, where it remains.

We strung lights across the big back deck of our Logan Square apartment, hosting parties and potluck dinners. We rented out the two extra rooms in our apartment, passed out keys to our friends, stayed up late drinking and partying and listening to music and having sex. We started dating other people, too, and we'd spend nights away from home and then come back together in the mornings. Those were my favorite moments: one of us would be in the shower when the other returned home, and the other would peek their head into the bathroom, both of us smiling mischievously at each other and our good fortune, our freedom to fuck and play and return to the person you loved.

In the basement of the Chopin, this beautiful old theatre in Wicker Park, a remnant of Nelson Algren's Polish Chicago, bodies swirled in anticipation: sweaty, glistening, some half-dressed, others half-blitzed before the show had even started. Dina and I looked into the crowd.

"You have my passport?" she asked.

"In my pocket," I said. "You want some whiskey?" I asked, pulling out the flask we'd packed. She took a pull.

"I'm gonna get us more beer," she said.

People continued to stream into the basement of the Chopin. I watched Dina return from the bar with two PBRs stacked on top of each other. She snaked through the crowd, patting people on the forearms, giving hugs to acquaintances like they were close friends. I envied her in those moments, the ease with which she moved through this world. She stopped to talk to Chris—a tall, handsome man, the lead choreographer of the show, and the other guy she'd been dating. He had broad shoulders and rugged features. He wore suspenders over a bare chest.

Nicholas Ward

Dina returned.

"How's Chris?" I asked.

"He's good," she said. "You should say hi."

"Nah, I'm okay."

"You should really get to know him. He's a good dude."

I shrugged, popping the top off my beer. "Yeah—but no. I don't know. It's weird."

Dina put a hand on my knee and made sure to look me in the eye. "It's only weird if you make it weird."

It wouldn't be the first time I'd made it weird. Earlier that summer, I'd gotten blackout drunk at a party and shouted, "I want to meet Chris!" Dina was displeased—even more so when I insisted that she come home with me. We did eventually meet, Chris and I, taking shots together at another bar in a different section of the same neighborhood.

I understand now that Dina and I were navigating difficult spaces. We had a domestic life but two roommates. We worked opposite schedules, and we were on different trajectories. It was my last summer before leaving a full-time job in the theatre and I had no idea what I was going to do. It was the last few months before she had to get a full-time job, as money from a grant she'd received was running out. I'd been really anxious, especially in public spaces, and especially when Chris was involved. I wonder now if my anxiety stemmed from a tension between the kind of person I thought I was supposed to be—a dutiful careerist with a one-track mind and a monogamous partner—and the person I was becoming. Before we left for the show, I admitted to Dina that I was nervous about going to this party. She told me I was being dramatic, which I didn't think was very fair. I knew my anxieties were valid, especially those moments when they took over my whole body. But I didn't want to start a fight; I didn't want to dig into the fissures that were forming around our relationship. I wanted everything to be easy, even though I knew that easy lived far apart from us. So, I buried my feelings and went out for the night.

After the show, we dispersed. Stage managers cleared space, moving chairs, adjusting set pieces, while the audience and performers, sweaty and euphoric, chorused into a dance party. I made my way to the center of the dance floor where I tried to lose myself amidst the crowd and gallons of cheap beer I'd drunk. It wasn't taking. Everyone was young and alive and free and drunk, and I realized that maybe I wanted to be at home reading a book.

I found Dina, strawberry-blonde curls piled high atop her head. She was talking with Chris, caught in a smile.

Chris turned in my direction. "Hey man!" He gave me a sweaty hug.

"Great show!" I said.

"Thanks," he said. "It's been a wild couple of weeks."

I turned to Dina, who was bouncing on the balls of her feet. Her smile had disappeared.

"I'm gonna go," I said, leading her slightly away from Chris. "I'm not having any fun."

"Is everything okay?" she asked.

"I'm just over this night. You're gonna stay?"

"We're going to the Continental," she said.

"Oh," I said, allowing this information to wash over me, that she'd made plans without me already. "Remember, we have auditions in the morning." I was helping her cast a play.

"I know," she said.

"Well, you're an idiot if you stay out late."

She smiled. "Don't worry about me."

With a nod to Chris, I pivoted and left.

It was a brief train ride home up the Blue Line from Wicker to Logan. As the car rumbled, all the drunks packed into the same car, I wondered what Dina and Chris were doing without me. I was dating someone else too, a dancer named Beth, but I wasn't settled in it. Dina seemed to float through the world with ease. I was concerned when she stayed out all night without telling me, worried that she was putting everything else before me and unsure if we could really make this relationship work. I was wrapped up in my feelings, but I didn't know what to do with any of them.

By the time I got home, I felt better. I hadn't freaked out; I wasn't anxious. I had identified a problem and found myself a solution. I went to sleep.

I woke with a start to the back door slamming. I looked at my phone. An hour had passed.

Dina threw open the door of our bedroom, eyes on fire. "You have my fucking passport," she snarled.

I sat up. "Shit," I said. "You're right."

"I was standing outside of the bar with Chris and everyone from the show, and I realized I couldn't get in."

"I'm really sorry," I said. "I totally forgot that I had it."

"That's such bullshit," she said. "Did you do this on purpose?"

"Of course not," I said, on my feet now and angry myself. "I did the right thing! For once! Can't you see it was an accident?"

"It doesn't feel like an accident," she shot back.

We fought long and hard that night. The next morning, we laughed about having a stupid fight over a silly thing, but something had cracked open, some fissure that had been sitting just under the surface. It was only a matter of time before the dam burst open.

On Labor Day, Dina met Chris for lunch at Reno. I sat on the couch in our apartment reading, windows open, sunlight streaming in from the boulevard. I'd just worked my last week at my job, and I was excited to wait tables again. I was also fired up about a solo trip I'd bought myself to New Orleans.

Dina called on her way home. "Chris broke up with me," she said, her voice shaking. "I don't want to talk about it, but I wanted you to know that I'm really upset."

She returned and sat on the back porch with our new roommate, James, her best friend from college. I kept my distance, but it ate me up inside that I couldn't be the one to make her feel better.

Later, she told me everything. "He was quiet at first." We were facing each other, Dina wrapped in a quilt, her eyes bloodshot from crying. "And then he said he couldn't date me anymore. When I asked him why, he told me that he loved me." She started crying. I remained silent, but my heart raced.

"I love him too," she said, tears rolling down her face. "But he doesn't want to be a part of this. He just wants me."

I reached out a hand. "There is a way you can be together if that's what you want."

She shook her head. "No. You are like oxygen. You're like gravity."

In New Orleans the next day, I stopped for a drink at a bar on the outskirts of the French Quarter. I wrote Dina a note on a cocktail napkin and sent her the picture. It read: "If you and Chris love each other, I want to support that. I can only celebrate more love in the world." If I was like oxygen, then I would do my best to breathe with her.

One night, later that fall, we both drank a good deal of wine at an art gallery. It was the first time we'd actually been around each other socially in weeks, not passing by each other on our way to work. I was tense about the conversations we both knew we needed to have. Guzzling wine appeared the surest balm.

In the cab on the way home, I confronted her about the shift I'd felt in our relationship, how it seemed like she was struggling to fit all facets of herself side by side: the dedicated artist next to the committed partner in an open relationship.

She agreed. "I don't want to go down this path and close all other avenues," she said.

"Nothing is closed, Dina. But it takes effort."

"It's so hard," she said.

"No shit. But you have to want to do it—in your heart. Not a checkbox on a to-do list. You have to want to spend time with me in the same way you love scouring the internet for image research."

Nicholas Ward

"But that's my work," she said.

"This is your life, too," I said.

She shifted in her seat. "I've been thinking about this recently, and I think I need to go away for a few days, to stay at a friend's place, to clear my head, to decide what I really want."

I stewed in silence. How could she still not know?

We found ourselves on the back porch, more wine open. It was October but warm still, and we relished our final moments of outdoor time. We eased into the cheerful familiarity that I loved about our relationship. I told her about a sex move Beth performed that I surprised myself by liking; she said she might get drinks with Chris. And then she began spitballing about pursuing a high-profile job opening in New York, whether or not it made sense to leave her blooming career in Chicago and move to the East Coast like she'd always envisioned.

"Would you want me to move with you?" I asked. If she said yes, I told myself, then we could figure out all the messy details of our life.

She took a breath. "I don't know." It wasn't no, exactly, but it was confirmation to me that we were falling apart. We had our biggest fight then. Actually, it wasn't even a fight, more that I found myself on the brink of brutality before focusing my anger on her years of hard work, scattering those pages far and wide until our home looked like something out of the final act of a play.

The breakup happened in stages. After my outburst, she disappeared, she came back, she ended it, then she didn't want to break up but wanted separate rooms, so I moved into the spare room to give her space. Then she went away again, then she came back and definitely didn't want to break up, so I celebrated by having Beth over for dinner and slept with her in my bedroom— the spare room, my room—but that was evidently not okay, not cool at all, not keeping with the terms of whatever it was we were doing.

The day Lou Reed died, Dina slunk around the house listening to "Heroin" on repeat, the druggy death rattle shaking the walls of the apartment. In the evening, I came home from an event I'd produced to find her on the couch watching a TV show on her laptop. I tried to snuggle up and watch the show with her.

"I'm still super pissed at you," she said.

"I know," I said, even though I didn't really understand why.

She paused the show and closed her computer. "I can't do this," she said. "And it's not fair to you, but I'm going to ask you to move out."

I took a breath. "No fucking way."

It was a hard winter: cold even by Chicago standards, and impossible to find an apartment I could afford, something temporary, something where I could stash my books and my cat for a few months before hoping to disappear.

After one evening of looking for lodging where the best option was the basement room of an underground and off-the-books cinema house with no windows, I came home deflated.

Dina was working in her bedroom. It was all hers now. She'd rearranged it to accommodate a new desk, and it was almost like I'd never lived there, never put my clothes in the closet or piled books on an end table before I went to sleep.

"I know how hard this is for you," she said. I'd decided to move out after all. I had the money, and she didn't.

"Do you?" I asked.

"Yes," she said, lowering her face to stare at her desk. "I really do."

"What about gravity?" I asked. "What about oxygen? Were you lying the whole time? Are you ever going to tell me why you broke up with me?"

She looked at me with tears in her eyes, but I felt no softness toward her, no care.

"I can't," she said.

I slammed the door in her face. In my room, I pounded my

desk and screamed as loud as I could. When I moved out, I figured I'd never see her again.

Finally, it was spring again. The coldest Chicago winter in two decades was thawing and my heart went along with it. I lived in an apartment with two people I can't imagine not in my life. Improbably, I'd fallen in love again. And I'd booked a one-way ticket to Europe.

Dina and I met for lunch a few weeks before I left.

"Get a beer," she said when I sat down. "We're gonna need it."

A year before, almost on the exact same day, I'd moved into her big, beautiful apartment. There had been so much hope back then. Now we were nothing.

I was gruff with her over lunch. When she asked about my trip, my new girlfriend, I didn't reveal much. I always thought it was Dina who didn't try hard enough to keep the relationship alive, but as we finished eating, she said, "You were so awful to me."

"When?" I asked.

"The whole month before you moved out," she said, like it was the most obvious thing in the world. "The whole month before we broke up."

At first, I argued with her, making my case. But the more we talked, the more I saw how the screaming, the door slamming, the unkind words, the trashing of her things was a violence. I thought I had a right; I thought I was simply reacting to and expressing the machinations of my heart.

"Are you ever going to tell me why you did it?" I asked.

Dina looked off behind me, where a wall of televisions played sports highlights in the empty bar. Her eyes welled. "I felt trapped," she said. She allowed a weighed breath to escape from her lips. "Ending our relationship was the hardest thing I've ever done."

I took a sip of my beer and set it down. I looked at her, and I tried to listen.

All Who Belong May Enter

We're driving down Freedom Road in my parents' blue Buick, Mom and Dad in front, my girlfriend and me in the backseat, like some pristine, suburban foursome. Nima nibbles on our afternoon snacks while I thumb through glossy food magazines. Today is my mom's birthday. All morning, she's been flitting back and forth around the house getting ready, mixing expressions of joy to be spending the day among friends, her son, and his girlfriend with despair over the season's closing of the swim club.

"I'm so sad it's closing today," she says for the fourth time already.

"I know, Mom," I say, annoyed. Nima presses my knee with her hand, a reminder for patience.

My dad steers the Buick into the pool's parking lot, resting under a covering of trees. It's not too crowded, but the club has only just opened for the day.

"Okay kiddos," he says, "make sure you bring everything." He likes using this moniker for us, this reminder that he's still my dad. I'm thirty-three, the same age he was when I was born. Unlike him, I'm still restless about my life's trajectory. Nima is my third long-term girlfriend in six years. While I envision a future with her that never materialized with the previous two, I don't think I'm living the life my parents imagined for me.

"You ready for this?" I ask Nima, scooping up our bundle of towels and snacks.

"Should I be scared?" she asks.

I'm a little on edge. This is the first time I've brought her home for the weekend. We grew up very differently. Nima was born in New York to a Pakistani family, raised in Boston, grew up Muslim, Ivy League educated, and has lived in Pakistan, Jordan, Germany, Bosnia and Herzegovina. I'm white and she's a person of color. I'm straight and she's queer. I'm thirty-three years old and she's twenty-five. In Chicago, our differences don't seem to matter. Here, I worry they might be magnified.

My dad signs us all in at the front desk and pays the guest fees. I don't remember there being a fee when I used to come here with my friends.

Nima starts to follow me through the men's locker room. "Sorry," I say, "you have to go through the women's side." I gesture behind her to the opposite showers and tiled rooms that snake around and exit onto the pool's deck. She shoots me a look of disappointment. I shrug; gendered locker rooms are par for the course here.

The Farmington Glen Aquatic Club, The Glen, looks just as I remember: an L-shaped pool, six lanes wide, the depth traveling across from three feet to five feet before giving way to the twelve-foot deep end under the lone diving board. The pool is surrounded by a pavilion offering ping-pong and snacks with a basketball court, volleyball net, and small field farther back. It's shabby, less well-manicured than I recall. I also haven't been here in fifteen years. Growing up, I loved the stultifying summer days with my friends when we were bored with nothing better to do and nowhere to go; we could always come here.

"We sit here," my dad says, walking past me and gesturing to a group of pastel blue lawn chairs just off the women's locker room.

"We sit in the shade," my mom says, adjusting her floppy pastel hat, "but you should sit in the sun." She points toward the diving board at the other end. I can't tell if we're not invited to sit with them or are being encouraged to enjoy the day how we see fit. Probably the latter.

We're introduced around: to the Davises, who I've known since birth, and to the Vraneks, who share goat cheese and apricot hors d'oeuvres they brought; and then we just stand there, awkwardly bouncing on our feet, wondering if our presence is needed any further.

"Okay, you're released," my dad says, his head already buried in his Kindle. My mom has begun gossiping with her friends. I smile at how my parents settle into their routines. I wonder if this life is in store for Nima and me.

We turn and begin the long walk to the deep end of the pool.

It's not that crowded yet, barely past opening, but everyone —ladies my mother's age chatting, children splashing in the water, young couples with toddlers—seems to watch us. As we walk past the rows of lawn chairs, our sandals smacking on the stubbly concrete of the deck, we keep our eyes focused forward. Every single face, like mine, is white.

We arrange ourselves by the diving board, spreading out our towels and magazines. Nima slowly removes her colorful dress to reveal an off-white bikini. She crosses her arms over her chest. "Everybody is staring at me," she says.

"It certainly looks that way," I say. There are maybe fifty people here. No one makes direct eye contact, but I can feel

Nicholas Ward

their attention. It's something I'm more attuned to now, how these looks can show up and damage the people that I love. Of course, The Glen is not officially an all-white space, but it's a private pool in a Detroit suburb that's still majority Caucasian. An interracial relationship is uncommon here.

"Also, we're not married, and we don't have kids," I say. It's a lame excuse, and I know it.

I keep scanning the pool. I see my mom flutter from group to group like a glad-handing politician, saying hi, laughing, pointing in our direction. I wave.

"I didn't understand why your mom wanted to come here on her birthday," Nima says. "I thought it was like going to the gym or something. But now I get it."

My parents have been members here for almost thirty years. When I was four or five, they decided it would be a nice way for us to spend our summers. As a kid, I hosted my birthday parties at The Glen and participated on the swim team, racing against kids from the other private clubs in the area. I even won a race once, though I didn't advance to the finals. When I became old enough to ride my bike on my own, and eventually drive, it became the summer destination. I drank my hooch here, a Kool-Aid-based concoction mixed with all manner of hard alcohol pilfered in small doses from my father's liquor cabinet. In high school, I snuck in after-hours with my friends on staff to drink beer and go skinny dipping, but I haven't actually set foot inside the grounds in fifteen years. It's my parents' pool now. They pay $600 a year for the privilege of attendance between Memorial Day and Labor Day. It's an astonishing figure to me. I can't imagine paying an extra 200 bucks a month in the summer just to go swimming. In Chicago, there are public pools available for free, not to mention Lake Michigan. Here in Oakland County, there are nine private aquatic clubs just like The Glen. In terms of free options, while there are beaches spread throughout the region's nine hundred square miles, there are just two pools and a handful of splash pads. In Detroit, there are even fewer.

A familiar refrain pumps over the loudspeaker. "It is now two o'clock and time for adult swim. All children under the age of eighteen must leave the pool." The games and splashing cease as the kids, with a minimum of grumbling, lift themselves out of the pool. They scamper off to the snack bar, to the field behind us, running and gliding while the adults take to the pool.

A small boy, five years old, stops at our lawn chairs. He's fantastically blond, shockingly so, eyes as blue as the sea. He knits a furrowed brow in Nima's direction. He seems transfixed by her, his pupils unwavering from her body. He almost hovers, like he's floating on air, eyes cascading over her brown skin.

A split second later, he's gone, back into the mass of children.

Nima shoots me a what-the-hell look. I shrug. I've no idea why that barely sentient being thought he could walk up to a stranger and stare. Everybody else is doing so from far away.

"I'm going off the diving board," I say. "Wanna come?"

"No," Nima says. "But I'll watch you from the water."

On the diving board, where I used to attempt flips, I bounce as high as I can. I keep my frame thin and compact, allowing my body to shoot towards the bottom of the pool twelve feet below.

I crest to the surface, shaking the water off my head, throwing my hair back.

"I'm going again!" I shout to Nima, watching from the pool.

"Come swimming with me," she says, treading water.

"I wanna try a cannonball!" I shout.

"You're silly," she laughs. "Hurry up!"

Infected by this giddiness, we completely undermine the point of adult swim. Everybody else is dutifully moving in specific lanes, but we refuse: staying close together, arms around each other, laughing as we momentarily drown one another while attempting piggyback rides.

My parents love it. "Knock it off you two," my dad shouts in that way he does where it seems like he's being mean, but

209

he's actually joking. "You're so cute," my mom calls as she glides past us.

If the older adults are annoyed with us, if they can't wait to get back to their seats and grumble about the kids with no respect for order, they don't say, and we don't care. We're expressing joy in ways often discouraged in adulthood, and we both love that we've found this in each other.

"You two looked like you were having fun!" my mom says after our time's up. With her is Mrs. Latham, a minute blonde woman I've known since childhood. Hiding behind her thigh is —I'm guessing—her grandson, her oldest daughter Laurel's kid.

"Hi, Mrs. Latham," I say and introduce her to Nima. "And who are you?" I inquire to the boy, craning my neck to peek around Mrs. Latham.

"This is Jeremiah," she says, lisping a little through her braces, bending to talk to her kin. "Jer, can you say hi to Nick and Nima? You can say 'Nima', right? It's kinda like Nemo! He loves that movie," she continues to us, too busy bothering with him to notice that I've frozen. Did she really just compare my girlfriend's name to a cartoon fish?

I look to Nima. She's sitting with her legs crossed, hand over her mouth. She's trying to smile, but it's a pose I've seen often. She is flustered and uncomfortable and wants everyone to leave her alone.

Oh, for fuck's sake, I want to say, *it's a pretty fucking recognizable name throughout the world.* But I'm aware we're visitors in this environment, even though I grew up here. I can grumble about it at home, but at the pool, everything remains breezy and surface-level. I'm also conscious that any battles over the pronunciation of her name are my girlfriend's to fight even though I'm sure she wouldn't be comfortable doing so here.

When they all finally leave, Nima takes a deep breath. "Your people are so weird," she whispers.

I make a big show of reacting, throwing my hands in the air, gesticulating wildly, "Whoa, whoa, whoa—these are NOT my people!" She laughs, riling me about the looks we continue to draw from our neighbors on the chairs.

"They are so your people," she says again, giggling, because she's right and I know it.

"Do you rebel against the suburbs?" she asks when we've calmed down.

"I want to," I say. "But I don't know how." I can reject the suburbs, but the suburbs will never reject me. Being white and middle-class means that I can dip in and out of here whenever I please. I can only imagine Nima's exhaustion in this world. I cannot experience it.

The pool has filled up, no space for seats anywhere on the deck. A game breaks out during the next adult swim. Some fathers have started cannonballing off the diving board and splashing their children, tremendous explosions of water the kids receive with unfettered joy. Pretty soon the dads—and some moms, too—are lining up, spurred on by their offspring, soaring in the air like superheroes. The line at the board gets longer, and at every "go," the kids chant, "Cannonball! Cannonball!" The whole pool is watching, adults laughing at these men and their children. Nima is smiling wider than I've seen her all afternoon. We both are.

"There should be judges," she says.

"Nah, we all know who would win." I nod to the man with wide shoulders and red shorts, whose attempts send a chorus of rousing cheers and high-pitched squeals from the kids. He's stepping onto the plank now like a big-league slugger, surveying the board, marking his jump. He leans back and takes off, all 200-plus pounds of him springing off the board, jackknifing through the air, hewing close to the deck so he can spray the line of children hopping there, waiting with baited enthusiasm for him to collide with the water.

Nicholas Ward

Nima whispers in my ear. "Look, there's another person of color!" Standing in line for the cannonball contest is a Black man about a decade older than me.

He gets up to the diving board and, I swear, for a fraction of an instant, a hush comes over the crowd. It seems to me like the clapping isn't quite as loud, the laughter muted, the squealing subdued. For the first time all day, we get a wide-angle perspective on the way they've been looking at Nima: examining her, silently questioning me for bringing her here. We watch the pool watch him. It's a persistent gaze that will never go away. Not here.

He jumps. He splashes. The waves explode. The children scream.

Later, in the car, driving home down Freedom Road, the sun shining through my parents' blue Buick, my mom asks, "Did you have fun?" I look across the seat to Nima, whose head rests on the window of the car, worn out from the day. I grab her hand. We don't respond.

Neither of us knows what to say.

How to Become
(and Stay) Sex Positive

In the bathroom down the hallway, I took off my clothes. Candles flickered around me. I changed into a fresh pair of red boxer briefs, balling up the rest of my clothes and stuffing them into my backpack. I wasn't sure if I was supposed to be wearing something more sophisticated.

I looked in the mirror.

I like my body well enough. I'm skinny and toned without being muscular. I have bags under my eyes, but my glasses hide them. I'm vain about my hair and make sure it's well-coiffed. And I have a competent cycler's ass honed from years of biking through Chicago.

I looked ready. I guess. Right before I opened the door, I felt a wave of anxiety overtake me.

Nicholas Ward

On the other side, where my girlfriend Nima waited, I could hear the sounds typical of any party on a Saturday night in Chicago: music and laughter, voices raised above one another, people entering to jovial greetings. I love parties, I really do—I love getting sweaty and drunk and flirty, bodies of people I know and people I don't nudging together.

But this party promised something new, something far more exciting than any party I'd ever been to. Still, I worried: what if I wasn't supposed to be there after all?

Nima waited in the hallway. Her hair fell over her forehead, concealing a few of her lashes. She wore a red bra I'd never seen before and black panties, and she sparkled with happiness. She leaned into me and planted a kiss on my mouth.

"Are you ready to hear the rules?" she asked.

My first kiss happened at a Lions football game with my dad. One Sunday, we sat next to the drunkest woman I'd ever seen in my life. She careened about the pavemented walkway in front of us, hardly sitting down. I was fourteen years old. She must've been in her forties. She wore big-framed glasses, with wavy brown curls of hair in the front and on the sides. She didn't watch the game, only cheering when everyone else did.

The Lions scored at some point, and the whole stadium rose to its feet. The woman grabbed my face and shoved her tongue in my mouth, moving it around my lips. She tasted of stale beer and cigarettes. She lingered there for a minute. I pulled away, panic-stricken.

"Switch seats with me," my dad said. He shot the woman and her companions a look. They muttered something about "not being very friendly." That's all we ever spoke of it.

That wasn't how I pictured my first kiss. Like most teenagers, I was sex-obsessed. I masturbated each morning while thinking of the cute girls in my school, practicing my kissing on the shower tile. I imagined lying on a blanket in a field or dancing in a room filled with roses. I didn't know what we would do once we got to the part where we were supposed to do stuff together, only that desire would take over and lead us. But that's not the experience I got to have for my first time.

I wonder now how that first kiss affected me. In the teenage world, it seemed like everybody hurled themselves at each other with ease. It didn't help that my reference was Paul, who had sex on the last day of eighth grade. But I felt so uncertain of what to do with my body, how to be fully present in it, compared to everyone else.

The apartment was a rectangular slab in Wicker Park. At the kitchen counter, U-shaped with a faux marble finish, I opened a bottle of champagne I'd pilfered from work. Nima stood next to me.

"You see the guy with the silver beard and the glitter?"

I looked across the room to an older man with a big smile on his face, glitter plastered across his chest; his arm dangled around a friend. He looked so easy, so comfortable.

I turned back to Nima.

"Before you got here, he got us all together in a circle and led us in a ritual and explained all the rules. Are you ready?"

"I'm still a little nervous," I said.

"Why?" she asked.

"I mean—I've never done this before."

"I've never done this before, either."

"You don't look nervous," I said.

"I took molly," she said with a giggle. "You want some?"

"I'll stick with my bubbles for now," I said, pouring some into a solo cup.

"Baby, you don't have to do anything you don't want to do, okay?"

I nodded.

A woman wearing a lime green thong emerged from somewhere to applause from the party. We both turned to look.

"Tell me those rules," I said.

Nicholas Ward

"Okay. You can only touch someone if you ask them, and you have to specify the location on their body. So, if you want to touch someone's shoulder, you say, 'May I touch your shoulder?' and if they say yes, you can touch their shoulder, and if they say no, you can't; but either way, you say thank you. Same if you want to kiss someone. Do you agree to the rules?"

"I agree." I looked out from the kitchen counter onto a lofted common space, where people I didn't know were mingling and smiling. Everybody seemed like they were all on the same page. I realized that included me.

I was twenty-four when I met Em at a bar in the Gold Coast. She was glamorous, with red hair that she tossed around her head. We made out in a booth while the bar emptied around us.

In the years between losing my virginity and young adulthood, I had occasional mediocre sex. I didn't date in college. I was paralyzed by my crushes, and my few one-night stands involved a lot of are-you-in-or-are-you-out fumbling that finished a few minutes later when I did, ignoring—not even considering—what else my partner desired or needed. It's not that I wanted to ignore those young women or that I was so convinced of my prowess that I figured a few thrusts would do the trick. I didn't know how to ask what I should be doing to make the other person feel good.

All of that fell away with Em. She knew what she wanted and she knew how to get it and she knew how to coax from me a desire and confidence buried deep inside me. For the first time in my life, I talked with the person I was having sex with about what we liked and didn't like, where to keep the condoms, to both pee after we finished. I didn't actually know what I liked yet, so I had to listen to her.

"I like it when you take control," she said.

One night, we were driving down Sheridan on our way back from dinner on Devon. At a stoplight, without thinking, I threw the car in park, pulled Em towards me, and kissed her for as long as the light lasted. That it was spontaneous and sexual, and that it was coming from my own body, blew my mind.

"Oh my god," she said, head back against the window, stunned. "That was incredible."

The minute we got back to her apartment, we were rolling around on her bed, clothes everywhere, bodies plastered together. It was the first time I ever felt love associated with sex— but it scared me. I didn't think I could sustain a life like that, couldn't function with that much emotion coursing between two people. Rather than run towards that shocking goodness, after two months, I fled.

I broke up with Em the morning after a fight, a bad one, but still, just an argument.

"I thought you could handle it when things get hard," she said as she left.

I shrugged. "I guess not."

I was a stupid young man who had found a way into a deeper part of myself, had found a relationship that prioritized love and sex, and I closed the door on it.

Almost a decade and a string of relationships later, I met Nima. The first night she spent in my bedroom in Logan Square, she stuck her finger in my butthole during sex—and yes, she asked. I'm telling you this because as the years wore on, she would tell people when someone asked how we met.

"He made me roast chicken and I stuck my finger in his butthole and here we are." I loved watching the reactions on people's faces, as they struggled to determine if she was telling the truth, as they tensed against their own Midwestern propriety.

The first time Nima slapped me, she was on top. We knew we liked choking each other, and I'd mentioned that I wanted to see what being hit felt like.

She slapped me out of nowhere, her palm connecting with my cheekbone. My ears rang. The light from the street cascaded

Nicholas Ward

against the walls of her bedroom in Pilsen, like someone had turned up the brightness.

I let out a yell.

"Do it again," I said.

"You sure?" she asked.

"I'm sure."

Her eyes danced. She smacked me again. Not as hard this time but just as worth it.

Nima and I were a good fit. We worked jobs we needed, me at a swanky West Loop restaurant, her as a teaching artist, both of us pursuing our artistic dreams. With her, I learned to find more comfort in my body. If I came too quickly or lost my erection, I didn't spiral into deep shame. I realized that there were so many other satisfying maneuvers that could be done in the bedroom that didn't involve my penis.

The morning of the party, we had breakfast in her apartment.

"So, like, will people just be having sex at this party?" I asked. "Should I pack condoms?"

"I have no idea," she said. "Are you nervous?"

"Totally. Aren't you?"

"Baby, I'm nervous about everything," she said. "But if we're together, we can both hang."

The whole night was a spectacle. Everyone had underdressed to the nines: feather boas and bare asses and so much glitter. Bodies coalesced into a make-out circle on the ground, couch cushions pulled into the center of the room. Someone suggested that we go on the roof, and Nima and I scampered hand in hand up the steps. We pushed open the door to reveal a snow-covered landing. In the middle, a beacon in the distance, a small cabana shone in the February night, lit from within. Our bodies shivered as we ran barefoot across the snow, red boxers, red bra, black panties still our only source of clothing. Once inside, we felt the warmth of space heaters hit our faces and wrapped our legs in blankets.

A couple sat across from us. He had a thick, black beard and a black ponytail and a full chest of thick, black hair. She was the woman in the lime green thong, face full of freckles, and a red bob. With the soft light of the cabana flickering against the dark winter morning, the couple leaned closer. "You guys wanna take a shower with us?" the woman asked.

For a moment, Nima and I looked at each other. That look was everything: our sexual life, desire for exploration, nerves, even our whole future: moving in together and making a life and breaking up. All of it, in a split second, showing us the way.

"Yes," Nima said. And then we were out of the cabin and back across the wet snow and down the steps and ignoring the party and through the corridor and into his bedroom with its own private bathroom, and the water was running and she and Nima jumped in and they were making out and he and I were watching and then we were all on the bed; more molly emerged from somewhere, and I stuck my fingers into the powder, uncertain if I was being dangerous or sexy or cool but not caring, just going for it, trying to find whatever version of myself had been there the whole time, waiting to break free. Soon, all four of us were on the bed passing ourselves from person to person, first Nima and me, then the woman and me, then she and Nima while he and I watched.

The next morning, Nima and I awoke in my bedroom.

"Did you have fun?" Nima asked while I spooned her.

"Did that really happen?" I asked.

We laughed, great giggles as our bodies shook.

"I think I can still feel the molly," I said.

Nima turned to face me. "Can we do that again?"

Nima and I have been broken up now for many years. But occasionally, we still reminisce about the night we had a foursome.

Nicholas Ward

These days, I make sure to talk about sexual wants and desires with my partners. I ask the new person in my life if she will choke me during sex.

"That makes me nervous," she says. "What if I hurt you?"

"I'll ask you to stop and I'll tap your hand just like this." I reach out gently and touch her hand.

"What if I'm still nervous?" she asks.

"Then you definitely don't have to. I like being choked; I don't need it."

Belong Is Where I'm Home

It was a hot day in August when our rented U-Haul rumbled along I-94 from Chicago towards Ann Arbor. Amadeus yowled every eight seconds for the entire journey, his crate fixed between the seats. I drove, tense about navigating the large vehicle.

As I pulled off the highway, we eased onto a five-lane stretch of sprawl.

"Well, this is where we live now," I said.

Nima furrowed her brow. "This is way more suburban than I expected," she said.

In one day, we'd gone from Pilsen in Chicago to a suburban cliché: all the grocery stores and pizza joints, home furnishings, liquor stores, wine shops, post office, banks, gyms, and every conceivable fast-food joint known to humankind packed into a

Nicholas Ward

few blocks of mini-malls. The cat howled. I laughed.

"What?" Nima asked.

I wanted to say something about our dread for the place creeping in so early. "I just never thought I'd be back in Michigan."

We'd rented our apartment without seeing it, a square two-bedroom basement unit. Large windows provided light and Nima's friends—who would attend grad school with her—lived across the parking lot. My parents came over from Farmington, and Patti—resettled back in Michigan—brought a bottle of wine. We ordered pizza from a college town classic that put halal meat on cheap wheels, which meant that Nima could finally eat pepperoni and we'd be getting their pizza all of the time.

By Labor Day, we'd purchased Ikea furniture, put away dishes and books, hung posters about. It was the kind of gorgeous afternoon that make Midwest winters bearable. I spent the day coordinating a visit to Patti's grandpa's lake house with Nima and friends, but they had a meet-and-greet at a professor's home, and then Patti's grandpa got nervous about inviting additional people, and so, as the day wore on, I sat in the apartment alone in a leather chair, looking out the window at the passing cars. In Chicago, I'd be grilling meats at a friend's house or riding my bike along the lake. In Ann Arbor, I imagined all four people I knew having fun without me. The misery blanketed me.

When Nima came home tipsy from her party, twirling in a yellow sundress, her face fell.

"Babe, what's wrong?" she asked.

I burst into tears.

"I miss Chicago," I wailed.

She sat on the couch, and I slid my head onto her lap, feeling like a small child.

"Do you want a beer?" Nima asked, stroking my hair.

"No."

"Do you want to go swimming?"

"Maybe."

"What's going on?" she asked.

"I don't know."

"Are you sad that you moved with me?"

"No," I said, sitting up to face her. "I just think this is going to be harder than I thought."

We'd been in Ann Arbor a week.

In Pilsen, we smelled masa when we stepped out our door. At the school on Cermak, boys played soccer under the bronze and lavender sun. In the summer, kids gobbled paletas off food carts and busted open fire hydrants. We lived in a big, cheap apartment on Blue Island Avenue.

Anywhere we made our home would be complicated. I moved to Pilsen because that's where she lived. If I'm being honest, I had rarely been to the neighborhood in the ten years of living in Chicago: once for a play, another time for a new restaurant, and a few summers before, to visit the National Museum of Mexican Art. We'd been dating for a year when I moved into her apartment. The neighborhood had changed from what it had once been, a working-class Mexican community. Now condos loomed over the 16th Street viaduct, Dusek's had received its Michelin star, the BowTruss on 18th got tagged with anti-gentrification graffiti. We promised to keep it local, to shop at Casa del Pueblo for groceries, go on dates at Plzen, have coffee at La Catrina. But when I stepped outside, it didn't matter where I spent my money. It mattered what I looked like. It mattered what I portended.

We lived above a gallery space in that apartment on Blue Island Avenue. Paper-thin walls meant sounds from below wafted into every room. If you were in the bathroom on the second floor, someone's blathering from the first floor felt like it was over your shoulder. I appreciated the parties for the variety of music but found the way it disrupted my sleep patterns stifling.

One wintry Saturday night, I became engrossed with a football game. A tense contest throughout, my spirits soared when my team punched in the game-winning touchdown. I leapt in celebration, pounding my fist on the floor.

I heard a knock at the door.

It was Arturo, manager of the space below.

"Is everything okay?" he asked.

"Absolutely," I said.

"I heard a lot of pounding, and I have clients from Wisconsin, and they're really concerned."

I should have let it go.

"Are you serious?" I asked. "People party down there all night, and you're actually complaining about a little noise at 10 p.m. on a Saturday?"

"But I have clients from Wisconsin, and I want them to book space here—"

"I know," I said, as I watched him shift on the balls of his feet, glancing back down the steps, "but please understand where I'm coming from. I'm just excited about a game."

"The landlord said I could operate that space—"

"It doesn't matter," I said. In an instant, I watched something flash across his face. I didn't know what it was in the moment, but later I realized it could've been fear, the fear of what might happen if I lodged a complaint.

"If you want," he said, "we can talk to the landlord next week."

"No," I said. I didn't want to start a fight. "You're right. I'm sorry. I'll keep it down."

The next day I slipped a note of apology into the door of the gallery; whether or not I felt like I was right or wrong didn't matter.

At the time, I thought we had to find ways to live with each other, but that wasn't quite right. I wanted to find a way to absolve myself of the ethics of living there. I didn't really need to establish a relationship with Arturo. I wanted to convince myself that I wasn't the same as the white people who buy condos and then call the police on families performing the same Sunday rituals they have been for decades. I didn't want to take over the community. I wanted to live within it. But I know now that's not really how gentrification works.

On a Saturday afternoon in late September, I drove Nima to campus before going to work. It was a home football game, the village nearly doubling with crowds in the Big House. The streets of the quaint downtown teemed with people buying memorabilia from trinket shops, falling drunk out of bars, weaving in and out of the crawling traffic.

"I don't understand it," Nima said to me as we inched along the tree-lined main street.

"I don't either," I said. But I did, at least a little bit. I rarely dressed up and tail-gated on big game days, but I've definitely organized my schedule around being able to watch sports.

On the sidewalk, a group of young white women—maybe college students, maybe recent grads—walked past us, decked out in the Wolverines' maize and blue.

"Ann Arbor is so cool," said one of them, throwing her arms aloft and turning back to her friends as she staggered along.

Nima and I looked at each other and laughed.

"Damn, this place is really in awe of its own ethos," I said.

"That's exactly what it is," Nima said.

After I dropped her off, I drove to the north side of town for my serving gig at a French bistro. The restaurant was upscale, located in a mini mall near the med school. Nearby tenants included a Turkish café, a Syrian bakery, and a sleek Indian restaurant. The place had been open a month, and well-dressed older white people would walk in and say, "It's just so nice to have a place like *this* nearby." I didn't know the area, but I could sniff out their meaning.

In Chicago, our lives spilled over into music and theatre and performance arts and food, taking us all over the city. In Ann Arbor, I went to work; she went to class. On nights we both had off, we made dinner and watched TV. It was a fine life, just not the one I envisioned.

One night, right before Christmas, we received a Whole Foods gift certificate from a friend.

"You want to spend it all tonight?" I asked when she suggested we go to the store.

"Yes," she said, "let's have some fun. Let's go nuts."

We bought scallops and shrimp and squid ink pasta. We bought fancy cheese and crusty bread. We bought wines I only usually dream of purchasing, two bottles at least. We cooked it all up that night, uncorked the wine while dancing in our kitchen. The new Childish Gambino album—*Awaken My Love*—had just come out, surprising us with its Funkadelic- and Ween-inspired meltdowns, and we blasted it. I made a feast: decadent seafood pasta with a lemony bite and Parmigiano-Reggiano over the top.

There was a party that night at one of Nima's classmate's basement apartments. One moment I was boisterous, talking with CJ about the Gambino album while Nima chatted with a colleague. The next, I sat on a rock outside crying. The simmering annoyance I'd been carrying towards Ann Arbor and my pathetic life exploded after the copious amounts of booze. "I'm miserable," I said to Nima, who I'd pulled from the party, making my meltdown her meltdown, making our lives all about me. We went home, and I raged more. I don't remember the context—still very drunk at this point—but at one moment I pounded the couch in anger and frustration. "You. Don't. Get. It." I yelled. But she did. Maybe more than I ever could.

I can see now that I didn't just hate Ann Arbor; I hated myself. I hated the way the town reflected my past back at me: that I had never changed, that I hadn't grown, that I hadn't really moved on.

One night in the late winter, well after dinner and right before bed, Nima had gotten up from the couch to use the bathroom. I continued to read my book. A bright light hit my face.

"Whoa," I said. "Can I help you?" I called outside. We'd only just started opening the blinds.

"Open the front door," the man behind the flashlight said, his feet at eye level. As my eyes adjusted, I saw a car idling in the complex's driveway and realized a young white cop was tiptoeing outside around our apartment building.

"Uh," I stammered, startled.

"Open the door," he said again, gesturing to the building's main entrance. His flashlight swung from the front door to our basement apartment.

"We're not going to do that," Nima called from the bathroom's entryway.

The cop bent down and looked at us like we were crazy. He gestured to his badge. "I'm the police," he said. He was four feet away from my face, separated by a single pane of glass.

"Sorry, but we don't open the door to people we don't know," Nima said.

"Seriously?" he asked.

I spun my head to catch Nima's eyes. We hadn't talked about it, but I knew we didn't need to.

"Yes," I said to the cop. "It's our policy."

"You gotta be kidding me," he said, backing away, craning his neck to the apartments above ours. Shortly thereafter, one of our neighbors came down for a brief conversation we couldn't hear, then he left. We agonized over our decision to not let him in. On the one hand, if someone in our building was in trouble, we wanted them to get help. On the other, we didn't know why the cop was there.

"We did the right thing, right?" I asked.

"I think so," Nima said. "This whole complex is people of color. We can't just put them in harm's way like that."

That was the first time I'd ever considered our surrounding space in Ann Arbor. It didn't seem like a city with neighborhoods. There was downtown, the university with its stately campus, and everywhere else. We never considered the politics of choosing a place to live in Ann Arbor; we were just passing through.

I wondered often what it meant to love Chicago. On return trips to the city, we always passed my favorite building, the Main Building of what was once the Armour Institute of Technology, which then became the Illinois Institute of Technology. It looms over the Dan Ryan, red like the color of clay, like the deep earth. It imposes its will on the land—no other buildings of its hue and stature nearby. I admire its heft, its accented window frames, the fire escape that shoots up an indented side piece. For the longest time living in Chicago, I didn't know what it was—which means I never bothered to look, its history hidden in plain sight. Will and I always marveled at it on our visits to Matt and Stefanie's in Beverly, like a checkpoint on our journeys south.

The building dates from the 1890s, unused now for decades. It's in the process of renovations to be turned into apartments, some of which they'll say are affordable, but I'm not confident. There's a bit of sick irony here: For sixty years in the neighborhood, from when my building was built until the early 1950s, thousands of Black Chicagoans lived in an overcrowded apartment complex known as The Mecca. The surrounding area, all the way down to 55th Street, became known as the Black Belt, the site of Black Chicago formed by the Great Migration and fortified by racist federal housing policy. When IIT acquired the land for their campus, they also took control of The Mecca and proceeded to deliberately refuse upkeep in order to create the conditions of something that looked like a "slum" which could then justify its demolition. In The Mecca's place, still standing, came S. R. Crown Hall, Mies van der Rohe's crowning achievement to mid-century design. The Main Building is the only one still standing from that era, and now it's going to be micro and one-bedroom market-rate apartments—the developer's words —that regular people probably can't afford.

I think about the past residents of The Mecca and their descendants. I'm sure some of them made their way to the public housing that the city built in waves on the State Street Corridor, homes named after Robert Taylor and Ida B. Wells. Most probably just had to make their own way. I'm not sure anyone knows for sure. What we do know is that the city of Chicago, under its Plan for Transformation, demolished the housing projects in the mid-1990s, and the Chicago Housing Authority promised the construction or renovation of some 25,000 homes in a ten-year period. They say they've completed this project, albeit ten years behind schedule, but on State Street, just 847 homes were built after 10,000 were demolished. It's staggering, what this city does to its most marginalized.

Maybe this is what it means to be white and love Chicago, to adore a building that represents a community's replacement. I wonder about the waves of hipsters, living in the gentrified playground of Logan Square. Will they know about the Mega Mall, where I bought my first work shirt for my first Chicago restaurant job, which is now a massive apartment complex with a Target on the first floor, only five minutes from another Target? Will they know about Helen's Two-Way Lounge, where Karen and I watched gentrification's uneasy integration take root, now a hip cocktail bar called Deadbolt? The land still exists, the centennial monument a beacon at the end of the wide boulevard. But the neighborhood is gone, and it's like this all across Chicago. The city has become a developer's dream, and one that is increasingly inaccessible to many. The changes seemed to spring up overnight though, of course, it's been in motion for years and began well before my arrival.

I consider the life I've led in restaurants and theatre, bouncing from neighborhood to neighborhood on a whim without consideration to what my living there might mean, and wondered how much I contributed to Chicago's destruction. I was a part of gentrification too—there was no easy solution for me to find a place to live and work. If there was a price for that I tell myself, I'd happily pay it, but I know it's far more complicated than that.

When Nima and I moved to Ann Arbor, we thought maybe this was the first step of the rest of our lives, that she'd get a tenured teaching job somewhere (despite those jobs disappearing) and I'd move along with her, finding work where I could. I realized quickly that I couldn't lose that tether to Chicago. I wanted to stay connected; I didn't want to be the kind of person who looked at the city and didn't remember.

One night in May, not quite nine months after we moved to Ann Arbor, Nima asked me to bring home a bottle of wine after work.

"What's going on?" I asked.

She was sitting on the couch, smiling wider than I'd seen her in months.

"Let's move back to Chicago."

"Really?" I asked.

"Yes! I hate it here; you hate it here. I brought you here, and I feel bad. We both miss Chicago," she said. "Let's get out of here."

"When?"

She laughed. "As soon as possible."

We made a list of the neighborhoods we wanted to live in, ranked in order of desire.

"Okay, what about Pilsen?" I asked.

"I don't think so," she said. "I just can't be a part of that."

"I think it's already jumped the shark," I said. "But if you feel that way, let's live somewhere else."

A few months later, we rumbled back into Chicago, cat between the seats yowling every eight seconds. It was the first day of July, a Saturday, and traffic was shit. But once we got onto the skyway, with a few middle fingers for Mayor Emanuel, we pulled onto the Dan Ryan with the city laid out before us, and we knew we'd returned to the right place. In many ways, that massive highway is a symbol of the racial animus, displacement, and segregation of this city: constructed during the era of a Democratic mayor as anti-Black as anyone who ever sat in City Hall and as racist as all the Southern whites the Midwest vilifies. We moved into Bridgeport, the Daleys' South Side neighborhood, once a stronghold of whiteness. But it, too, has changed. I like to think its lack of a racial majority, of hegemonic whiteness, would get Hizzoner rolling in his grave. After all, anything that pisses off a Daley, living or dead, is a worthwhile pursuit.

I Am Easy to Find

I sat in the bathtub and smoked. From my position in the bathtub, I had to raise myself out of the water, extend my right arm, and tap the end of the cigarette butt with my thumbnail into the sink. The water was lukewarm, the cleaning part of the bath long over. I don't even know how clean I actually got back when I used to smoke. These baths were an infrequent occurrence when I lived alone, a reminder that I controlled my surroundings, responsible only to myself. Getting clean wasn't the point anyway. Stanching my own loneliness was. Not that I ever did.

I was a junior in college, and I'd convinced myself that I needed to live alone. I'd grown up an only child, made my way without constant companionship, and fancied myself an independent loner. Being alone was a fact of my existence.

The year before, as a sophomore, four of my best friends and I lived together in a cramped dorm suite. There was always a friend around to get high with, have a smoke with, go for a walk. We took mushrooms on a cold, rainy night. Danced in our boxers to Gorillaz's "Clint Eastwood." Ate Matt's homemade sausages while high, laughing at how good they tasted. I didn't realize how rare that would be when I got older. Sitcoms about adult life that I watched growing up—*Cheers*, *Seinfeld*, and *Friends* —made it seem like life was a series of close interactions with people you cared about. Instead, I felt boxed in by the constancy of their presence. I needed to escape.

My first apartment was a squat thing, connected to another small unit with separate entrances, a white clapboard house on a corner lot with a sizable yard in front. It was nothing much: a small bedroom and kitchen with a long living space that allowed me to place two faded pastel couches from my parents' basement. The walls featured interior wood paneling straight out of the '70s. The only source of heat was a grated electric box in the middle of the room that roared to life with a fiery vengeance.

Before they left to return home to Michigan, my mom and dad drank beers on the couch. They didn't even seem to mind that I smoked. Mom gave me an old ashtray that once belonged to her mom. Dad left an acerbic away message on my answering machine.

Walking with my parents to their minivan on the day they moved me in, I waved to Jason and Chris, the two boys moving in next door.

"You know them?" my mom asked.

"Yeah, they lived in my freshman dorm."

"Well, that's nice you'll know someone right next door," she said.

"I don't know them that well," I said, shrugging it off.

I gave them both a hug, and then they were gone, and I was alone, as I'd always wanted to be.

The second week of school, on a Tuesday morning, Will nursed the makings of a black eye.

"What happened to you?" I asked.

Betsy cut in. "He's a fucking idiot is what happened to him."

Will shrugged. "Case race last night got a little out of hand."

"You guys had a case race?" I asked. "Without me?"

For months, since the end of last year, we had been planning a competitive drinking event where teams of two compete to see who can drink a case of beer the fastest—college binge drinking at its most unhinged. We had even planned the teams, Will and his roommate Keith, Aaron and Mol, me and Patrick (who would almost assuredly lose).

"Yeah, sorry," Will said. "We decided on a whim after class. Didn't even think to tell you."

"You're glad you missed it," Betsy said. As she went on to describe how Will and Mol got into a drunken fistfight, I stewed. Living alone didn't mean getting cut out of my friend circle. Years before FOMO made its way into the lexicon, I felt the disappointment of missing out.

That year was a slog. I cooked meals consisting of Rice-A-Roni and unseasoned pan steak. One night, I hooked up with a girl who stayed around the entirety of Sunday and seemed to want to move into my life, and I freaked out and ignored her calls the next week—an early version of ghosting. I spent many nights lying supine on the long couch and watching sports, waiting, and hoping that someone would call to hang out and knowing that I wouldn't make the effort to see anyone if they tried anyway.

I'm not sure I even knew how to define my loneliness back then—or even that I was lonely. I called it depression, but that doesn't seem correct either. I only know that I spent more time than I wanted by myself and I didn't know how to make the feeling of emptiness stop.

I never talked to Jason or Chris that year. Chris was a religious studies major who often referenced thinkers and philosophers I'd never heard of and couldn't keep straight, and saw no problem revealing the details of his sexual exploits. Jason was quiet; I didn't know him well, but he'd once dated a girl I crushed on, so I envied and disliked him for no reason. One cold night over winter break, I returned back to my apartment from work. I'd come back early from Michigan, a few days after Christmas, to wait tables and hang out until the semester started. I noticed a light on in Jason and Chris's apartment. I'd be lying if I said I thought about going over to say hello. Mostly, I was struck that someone else didn't want to be home with their family for very long.

That night, I found out later, Jason had come back from the bars and neglected to take his insulin; he'd gone into a diabetic coma and died. It was days before anyone found the body or thought to look. I never even saw anyone take him away.

I broke down when I found out, weeping in the middle of a cafeteria. I don't know if I could have saved Jason's life—probably not; I don't even know if the timelines aligned, if it was that exact night after all. But I know that a thin wall separated us and that neither one of us found a reason to scale it, and the thought of him dying alone triggered something in me.

In my first Chicago apartment, we'd been given leeway to paint, and I streaked my walls with bright blue and green lines, thickly applied. I told myself I was imitating Rothko, but really, I was just fucking around. Once I ran out of paint, I made a city-style scene on one wall and left the last one blank. It was a mess.

Our schedules were wildly different: Matt and I worked nights in restaurants; Will and Stefanie worked early mornings at cafes; Betsy found a stable nine-to-five. One night, Matt and I stayed out so late, we passed Will on his way to work. He was displeased with our revelry. That same evening, or maybe it was another, Matt and I went to the bathroom around the same time, and I took pictures of him posing sexily in Stefanie's white bathrobe.

It was everything I ever wanted for my new life.

At night, especially as late summer turned to fall, and then winter, my cat Amadeus would seek refuge under the covers from both the cold and Betsy's cat. He'd curl up into my body for warmth, and in the mornings, I would find him nestled in the crook of my torso, arms outstretched, large eyes looking up at me while purring loudly, as if to say, "You are mine and I am yours."

Amadeus had been the last of his brothers and sisters. They'd been rescued from a ditch by a woman who ran a doggy daycare. She fixed them all up and began parceling the litter out to other homes. No one wanted him. A year old, sleek and slender with tiger stripes on his back and white fur along the belly, he was too wild for anyone who came into contact with him. When I visited, he prowled around a small room, sequestered from the dogs, the only cat on the premises. He bounded over to me, nuzzled his cheek against my hand, and nibbled at my fingers. "He's the one," I said.

I'd grown up with an orange tabby named Marmalade. She came to us when I was five years old, the daughter of a neighbor's cat, one of five kittens. Marmalade was the only one who lasted into adulthood. She slept on my legs at night, licked at my face when I wore ChapStick, which I later recognized was pretty gross. She would beg to be let outside our one-story suburban rambler, and most summer days, she'd lounge in the grass, sunning herself. In the garage, she'd kill rodents: little voles that she placed on our carpet like a peace offering. When I left for college, Marmalade was thirteen years old. In the time that I spent away from home, her health declined. My dad was tasked with giving her weekly insulin injections, holding her down and massaging her belly while sticking a long needle into her flesh. She became senile, howling constantly, so loud that when my parents left me voicemails, I could hear her in the background. One day, when she was eighteen years old, she fell off the couch. My parents put her to sleep soon thereafter. My dad refused to go to the vet. He didn't want to watch her die.

When I think about the first years of my adult life, the images flash by. After Will and Betsy got engaged and moved out, Matt and Stefanie got a dog, a lovable beagle named Copa, before they, too, got engaged and began to build a life together. Once Amadeus and I started moving, it seemed like we would never stop. We found a tiny two-bedroom in Roscoe Village with my college friend Kathleen. When that landlord wouldn't fix a flooded basement and broken water heater due to a tornado, we moved again, to a three-bedroom nearby and picked up another old friend, Emily. A year later, Jay and Michael moved in; a year after that, Sam replaced Michael, and that period in my life is marked by revelry and laughter, by cookouts on the side cement walkway, getting high in the empty apartment above us, stumbling to the Black Rock bar ten paces outside our back door.

Around this time, I began to harbor a fantasy. Whenever I felt depressed, anxious and unsure of my place in the world, in my own damn life, I thought about getting in a car and driving. North to Wisconsin or Minnesota, or even west to one of the Dakotas. Hell, maybe I'd make it to Canada. I'd chuck my phone on the way out of town—it was all flip-phones back then—say a quick goodbye to my friends without telling them my plans, and Amadeus and I would start a new life somewhere else. I'm not sure what I'd do once I got to where I was going, how I'd even decide where to stop. Maybe I'd work in a bar somewhere and spend the rest of my days as a local, known about town for my eccentricities. I could do that in Chicago, of course, but something about the weight of balancing life as an artist and life as a waiter and life as a friend and a son and a boyfriend and maybe even a parent someday felt like too much to carry—never mind that many people carry far greater weight than that every single day. I was unprepared for the simple business of living, of being alive and paying bills, going to work and falling in love, making friends and never seeing some of them again. I didn't realize that all this existential malaise would follow me, no matter where I went.

Then I met Karen, my first serious girlfriend. Two years deep into dating, we found a one-bedroom apartment in Andersonville.

Nicholas Ward

The night we moved in together, in the blinding rain after a long workday, tired and frustrated, I let Amadeus loose. His nerves frayed, perplexed by the new smells of Karen's stuff, he bounded throughout the apartment and sprayed everywhere. We scrubbed the place mercilessly, but we only masked the smell. A base layer of urine covered everything and reeked, especially when the radiators cooked the place. I moved out six months later. When Karen and I started speaking again a year after that, she told me that she couldn't entirely mask the scent. For as long as she lived there, she felt our presence.

I never thought about living alone again. I convinced Jay to break his lease on the apartment we used to share—which had been overrun by slobs and pizza boxes—and moved back to Roscoe Village.

One night, when I was sleeping elsewhere, Jay got up to use the bathroom and heard meowing coming from the front of the apartment, near my room. Amadeus was standing on the window air conditioning unit, unable to get back inside. He'd climbed out of my window and onto the adjacent unit but couldn't figure out where to go next. Jay stuck his arm outside and grabbed Amadeus by the belly, pulling him to safety. "Never forget I saved your life," Jay would say to the cat whenever he saw him.

Back to Logan Square, completing some strange parabola of our lives. First with Dina, who wouldn't allow Amadeus into our bedroom. Then, after another breakup, across the wide boulevard where a new roommate named Erika welcomed us to live with her dog, Eva. A symbiosis formed between pit bull and feline; they never became friends, but they'd share space on the couch, a few moments at a time.

I sort of had a breakdown around that time, though I wouldn't call it such until many years later. I'd quit my dream job at Steppenwolf, and I was reeling from another breakup. I didn't know how I wanted to spend my future—the same bullshit as before, except now I was older. I didn't think I could stay in Chicago. I didn't think I could walk the same streets in the same neighborhood as Dina and not feel shame and guilt and sadness. And even though I'd started dating someone new, and even though I didn't know what to do with Amadeus, and even though I really shouldn't have cashed out my 401k that I'd spent the previous three years building, I did exactly that.

The summer I spent in Europe helped me to really appreciate being alone and also forced me to accept that I needed people. I spent the first month in Portugal, and it was miserable. I envisioned meeting people who would share my love of the world, my curiosity for the people in it, my desire to try new things. And I did meet those people. I also met incurious young men who only wanted to get drunk for cheap, couples with no interest in anyone outside of themselves, and older folks who had been floating through the world on a dime for decades and showed me a possible version of my future self I didn't want to see. But whomever I met, no matter how close of a bond we shared or how much I couldn't stand to be in their presence, every single person either left me or I left them, never to see them again. This gave me a slanted view on human relationships, at least at the start. If everyone you meet you'll eventually never see again, what's the point in even trying to find a connection?

I also felt shame from admitting that it was hard. What's hard about not working and seeing the world? What's hard when you can float through countries with ease? When the world is open to your body and accepts you no matter where you go? But hard is hard no matter who you are. And I was lonely.

One night, I took a bus from Sarajevo to Budva, Montenegro. We left around dusk, winding through the Dinaric Alps and down the coastline of the Adriatic Sea. Around midnight, at the first of four border crossings, passing into Croatia, the queasiness began. I angled my head against the window, propped against a rolled-up hoodie. Outside, the U-shaped customs building was cast in an ominous glow by one giant spotlight.

The agents stopped at a young man sitting in front of me. He boarded the bus in a small Bosnian town. I don't know if he was a Bosniak or not, but someone I met had told me the war wasn't really over; it was just on ceasefire. Maybe that's why he got pulled off the bus. He seemed nonplused, but as I watched him grab his bags and follow the border official into an office where a steel door shut, it sent a chill down my spine. Sweat poured off my face. I laid down on the empty seat next to me and closed my eyes. After some time—a few 'minutes? an hour?—the shaved-headed dude returned, and we lurched off into the night.

My stomach churned, sweat poured off of me, my heart rate quickened. Gingerly, I stepped to the bathroom and opened the door. No working toilet, no paper towels, just a repository for garbage with a putrid smell. Back at my seat, I fished out two tissues, dipped them into my water bottle, and plastered them to my face. It didn't work. I spun my head around the interior of the half-full bus. An older woman slept behind me while her daughter checked her phone across the aisle. I didn't have a choice, not really. I snatched the plastic bag linked along the armrest of my seat, buried my head into it, and barfed my insides out, chunks of the pretzels and cream-filled croissants that I bought at a roadside convenience store falling on top of discarded fruit and gum wrappers. When it was over, I tied the bag up, stepped into the bathroom, and chucked it into the sink.

It was in this moment that I realized there is no one to comfort me and how much I wanted that. In my sickness, I felt no one cared about my life. I texted Nima, even though we'd just started dating, but she was living her own life in Chicago, eating dinner with friends, or going on a bike ride. I was alone, just like I always said I wanted to be.

An hour after the first spell, I got sick again crossing back into Bosnia. And again, an hour after that, back into Croatia. I removed my vomit-flecked shirt and tied it up with the third plastic bag, pulling my hoodie over my head.

At three o'clock in the morning, finally, we arrived at the Montenegrin border.

I'm not surprised I got pulled off the bus. I was sporting a splotchy beard I hadn't trimmed in a few weeks, my unwashed hair was a disaster, and my pale face resembled someone who's just seen a poltergeist.

They made me take everything: my backpack, day bag, the tissues on my seat, the crumpled "Made in Detroit" T-shirt I'd retched on and removed, and the third plastic bag filled with vomit.

In a small room without windows, a customs officer stood before me.

"Do you have anything to declare for police?" he asked.

"Like what?"

"Like drugs," he said.

"What?" I asked again. "No, of course not." Couldn't he read the lines of my face, that I was scared and worn out and lonely?

He sifted roughly through my belongings, upending the care with which I packed my bag.

"Open this." He pointed to the bag of vomit.

"So you know," I said, "I've been getting sick." I gestured to my mouth. "Puking, you know?"

He muttered something to his cohort, who returned with two latex gloves.

I loosened the knot. He poked at it with his fingers, moving around a tissue before confirming that I wasn't concealing any drugs within my vomit. They let me go. I imagined the rest of the bus, tired and hungry and needing to pee as they waited for the dainty American who couldn't even hold down his dinner on a simple ride along the coast.

I vomited once more. Having used all the bags, I stood in the dark bathroom, projecting water into the chasm of the toilet below, the door swinging open behind me. The shaved-headed dude poked his head in, using his phone's flashlight.

"Are you okay?" he asked.

"No!" I shouted.

At 5 a.m., at the Budva bus station, I got off. I apologized to everyone around me, but I knew I'd never see them again. For the first time, that felt like a comfort.

The bus incident cracked something open in me. My final weeks of the trip, I began opening myself up to strangers. In Tirana, Albania, I ate sheep's head with a large group and explored the city with a blonde woman from Sweden. In Skopje, Macedonia, I met a Canadian named Josh who shared with me his own—far more harrowing—bus adventures. And in Budapest, Hungary, on my last night of the trip, I spent the evening drinking the last of my beers with a young Russian man, playing foosball and overlooking the balcony of our hostel. We talked for hours about the relationship between our two countries, places we wanted to travel, music we liked and didn't like. I never even caught his name.

This anonymity gave me comfort in a way it didn't before. I returned grateful that I got to experience the world in that way, not only its great monuments and artistic triumphs but also people I wouldn't be able to meet otherwise. It stoked a desire for travel that hasn't since abated.

When I came back from Europe, I reclaimed Amadeus from the small basement apartment where my friend Morgan had kept him —or I attempted to, at least. For weeks after getting settled back in my room, Amadeus couldn't be contained. He'd slip out my back door any chance he got into the open maw of the basement where boxes and luggage and books and old tables and a few decades of our landlord's life reigned. He sought Morgan's apartment, but he'd disappear into the clutter of the basement.

One night, while drinking with my roommates, I couldn't find him and gave up.

"What if he never likes me again?" I wailed to Nima.

"You just have to give him time," she said. "I still like you and you left me, too."

I shot her a look. She'd been joking, but not really, that I'd left her immediately after we started dating, but I always countered that I'd come back just to be with her.

Amadeus did find me again, and the following summer, we packed up our belongings and moved south to an apartment in Pilsen with Nima.

No one I lived with or dated loved Amadeus more than Nima. I tried not to resent it. When two creatures love one another, who am I to stand in their way? I'd return from work to find them sitting on the couch, Nima watching a show with Amadeus curled up on her lap. She'd suggest a half-hour afternoon nap, and after I would wake, they'd both carry on. I'd return from doing the dishes or writing emails to find Nima and Amadeus, he at her feet, or on her back, or tucked between the crook of her belly. That would knock me out, my two loves. Together. Serene. Beautiful.

Nima joked that he would live forever. "He will not live forever," I would say, with a little paternalism in my voice. She'd pout, "Don't say that!" We both knew that she knew that he wouldn't make it for all time, but she hated that I spoke the truth out loud.

We became the kind of people who talked about our pet in mixed company, like it was a child, telling stories that only we found funny. We hosted gatherings, friends crowded around a large sectional couch that opened into a bed. Amadeus would always join us, sitting on the edge of the cushion. He wanted to be included in the action. We inched our lives forward, Nima and Amadeus and I, until it was difficult to remember ourselves before we met each other.

Still, we kept moving. When I look back, it seems like I hardly ever stopped packing boxes. First to Ann Arbor, so Nima could attend grad school. Ten months later, we packed up and moved back, settling into the bottom floor of a two-flat in the Bridgeport neighborhood. We lasted six months before the stress of our lives got to us. We frayed at the edges, and one day, we were going to Target, and the next minute, it was over.

For the first time in sixteen years, I was forced to live alone again. I did interview some roommates, but it didn't seem like a good idea. I couldn't imagine sharing space with anyone else. I was too old for that. Too stubborn. Too sad. Everything had failed, and I just wanted to be alone.

Around this time, I'd come home each day to find that Amadeus had taken a shit on the kitchen counter. This went on, every day, for weeks, until I started covering the countertops with aluminum foil, which he hated. I took him to the vet, but we couldn't figure it out without an expensive and risky invasive procedure. I put him on medication to see how he'd respond. He never got better. Maybe it was thyroid cancer. Maybe he was just old. Maybe he missed his cuddle partner, his body a reflection of his broken heart.

I have begun now to recognize loneliness as a part of being alive; our inability to translate our most authentic selves, the parts of us buried deep in our bodies, to the wider world conjures a feedback loop of fear, anxiety, displacement, and solitude. It's a wonder any of us ever have functional relationships. It's a wonder we don't fall into pits of despair, being unable to communicate who we really are.

Cats are perfect for this malady—at least, Amadeus was. Whenever I'd been lonely, from the time I graduated college until the time I moved out of the apartment Nima and I shared together, I always had Amadeus. I felt like he could sense my moods, that he could tell when I was down and needed comfort, that he could intuit when I was angry and required softening. I wondered if he could feel my heat, if he knew my body better than I did. I was never truly alone because I had him, curled on my lap while I read or watched television, perched on my desk while I worked. Begging for food in the morning before I'd wiped the sleep from my eyes. Basking in the sun while I cleaned.

When I moved to the North Side, Amadeus declined even further. He was a thin shard of himself. I knew it was the end, but I just couldn't do it. I wanted some sign to tell me that it was time, someone to help me make the decision. We called Nima one night via FaceTime so that she could say goodbye. The next night, Will and Betsy came over; they'd been my roommates when I first got him, had watched him for many years anytime I went out of town. While they were over, Amadeus howled in bloody terror and then shit on the floor. Will and Betsy have three cats of their own, so they've seen about anything a cat owner can handle. "I don't think he has much longer," Betsy said. A few days later, I called and asked her if she would go to the vet with me while I put him to sleep. He was fifteen years old, a fine age for a cat to last. I was thirty-six, with far more life left if my luck held out.

At the vet's office, there is a special room for dying. It's tucked away near the front desk. Blinds are drawn. It's dark. Soundproof. Quiet. I sat with my cat and Betsy while we waited. I held his frail body in my arms. He wailed. I took pictures of us together, our final photos.

The vet came in, and I laid him down on the table. He could barely move, his body thin and gaunt, his fur splotchy and unkempt. He had stopped cleaning himself weeks before. Someone once told me that if an animal can see their loved one before they pass, can look into their eyes, then the pain of expiring won't be so great. So that's what I did. I held his tiny paws while the doctor injected him, and I stared into his eyes. I had looked at him that close so many times in his life, marveling at our good fortune, our fine match together, softening with love for this strange and wonderful creature who had somehow befriended me for most of my life. I don't know if I saw him expire, if I could actually see life leave him, but one moment he was there and the next he was gone.

Later, after we'd left the office, tears wiped away, I posted a goodbye note on Instagram, and the calls started rolling in: from Erika, Eva the pit bull's human, my old roommate in Chicago, now calling from Los Angeles, Morgan, my best friend who had lost their cat a few months prior, McKenzie, calling from before her film premiere, whose own cat, Wi-Fi, had charmed half the world as well, all calling to offer condolences, all calling to tell me they knew what it felt like, to love an animal so deeply that it didn't quite make sense but was the only thing that mattered in this goddamn world.

Nima posted on Instagram too. She called Amadeus hers, and a part of me wanted to remind her in my grief that she didn't have a right to claim him, that she met him later in life, refused to clean his litter, that she left the both of us, wedging the country between. But that would be unfair. The heart knows no boundaries. I'm not disposed to start making them now.

After Amadeus passed, after I settled into my new apartment, after the conversations with Nima grew more infrequent, that's when the loneliness really set in. I felt hollow. I drank too much and watched movies, sitting in my comfy chair, berating myself for wasting an evening, spending my time the same way I would have if I lived with a partner or a friend. And I put entirely too much stock into my dating pursuits. I didn't even want a relationship. But I expected every person I went out with to be the cure for my loneliness, and I spiraled when it didn't work out. The bottom was a day spent working on an all-day Saturday event that my job produced. I had a coffee date the next morning, but when I reached out to confirm, she messaged back that it wasn't going to work out. Never mind that I have done that myself, never mind that she owed me nothing at all. It was proof that I was an abject failure if I couldn't even convince someone to meet me for coffee. Later that night, as the event wound down, I started pounding whiskey, and then more drinks, on a pretty empty stomach at the after-party next door whereupon I twirled some girl whose name and face I don't remember around a makeshift dance floor and practically begged her to come home with me, while all of my coworkers looked on. I spent the next day buried with shame until I came in on Monday and my colleagues thought I had been so much fun. If they couldn't even see the depths of utter despair, I guessed I could spend the rest of my life hiding it forever.

I don't exactly know how I pulled myself out of the great mess of my life, but I did. I put up boundaries at work, stopped making myself completely available at all hours to respond to whatever small missives that someone would think to send my way. I became active in scheduling hang times with friends, going to plays and readings. I dated some very nice people, women I didn't want to take a deeper step with but who, nevertheless, were pretty damn great. But mostly, I decided that this was my life, and I couldn't necessarily choose what happened in it all of the time, but I could love myself as I navigated my way through it. I could choose to love me. So, I did. For me, making that active choice to love myself is a daily practice that damn near saved my life. I know that healing is a constant process, one that men aren't taught to pursue. But so many of us are so broken, and we need to find our way back to love, or to love for the first time.

I wake up every morning, or most mornings, mornings when I've given myself a good night's sleep, not gotten too drunk or stayed out too late, allowed myself to breathe and not give in to my anxiety, to not think too deeply about what I want out of this life, and I write at my desk. I have coffee set and ready to go. I either write with a computer or by hand. My window looks out onto the building's courtyard, where I watch the seasons change. There's an oval-shaped green space in the center of the courtyard. It's fenced in, not wide enough to lie down in or plant an individual garden. There are a few trees, some flowers that I think might be

Nicholas Ward

nasturtiums or hyacinths, but I don't really know, not being prone to flowers. It's nice for what it is, a small patch of greenery in a city constantly dying under the swell of development. In the summer, I have the windows thrown open if it's not too hot. I prefer not to have air conditioning if I can help it. I like to watch the life of the courtyard begin to take shape: my neighbors leaving for the day, a maintenance man watering the trees and flowers, the birds flitting from ledge to ledge, the hum of AC, rabbits burrowing into the earth. Sometimes, after work, I take my fold-out beach chair down to the stoop, with maybe a glass of rosé or a gin & tonic, and read from whichever book has captured my attention. It's nice, this life that I made for myself.

I got a new kitten, a four-month-old shorthair named Soda. He was named before I acquired him, and in my flair for the dramatic, I rechristened him King Soda Cat the First. My life is full of constant regeneration, life and love and death and renewal. Maybe someday, when it's all said and done, I too will die with someone I love looking into my eyes.

Thanks

I'm aware of the cliché that every debut author will thank every single person they've ever met, every lover, friend, and optometrist, but I may never write another book again, so I'm leaning into that excess. I'm sorry if I forgot anyone.

First off, big thank you to Jaquira Díaz for selecting this book as the winner of the 2020 Autumn House Press Nonfiction Prize. *Ordinary Girls* was a lighthouse for me, and I'm honored and grateful for your support. Thank you to the entire team at Autumn House, especially Christine Stroud, who was a generous editor, who pushed when I needed it, and who helped me dig deep to find something more worthy of readership.

The Swarm Artist Residency was the first time I allowed myself to feel like an artist. I didn't get much writing done, but it helped pave the way for the book to begin. It's amazing to see what you all have built.

I try to push against the notion that being a writer is a single-minded pursuit. Nevertheless, writing every day in residency at the Ragdale Foundation made me feel like a writer for the first time, and it's where I started crafting the essays that would coalesce into this book.

Liz Rice told me in 2013 that I would have a book published before I turned forty. I didn't quite make the deadline, but I got very, very close. Thank you for believing in me.

I learned how to tell stories with 2nd Story, my artistic home for most of my adult life. Thank you to Matt Miller, who saw something in me as his intern; you are more of a mentor than you know. Thank you to Adam Belcuore for bringing an earnest young theatre maker aboard, even though it was clear I had no idea what I was doing. Thank you to Megan Stielstra, who has shown so

Nicholas Ward

many of us how to find our voices and who believes with every fiber of her being that the world needs our work. I wouldn't be a writer without you. Thank you to Amanda Delheimer, whose leadership has navigated so much, and who consistently impresses with her grace, acumen, and thoughtfulness. To Lauren Sivak, whose drive continues to elevate our organization to unseen heights. And to Molly Each, Khanisha Foster, Kimberlee Soo, Aimy Tien, Stephanie Chavara, Liz Blondel, CP Chang, Jess Young, Margaret Marion, Julie Ganey, Jess Kadish, Earliana McLaurin, LaTanya Lane, Megan Shuchman, Andrew Reilly, and so many more, in whose friendship and artistic fellowship I found an artistic purpose and learned how to listen.

To the friends I've made out of the sprawling Chicago theatre community, who deserve more than this city's institutions seem fit to provide. Many of you barely do theatre anymore, most no longer live in Chicago, and some will disagree with what I've written, but I appreciate you all the same: to McKenzie Chinn, Sam Bailey, Brian Golden, Tracey Kaplan, Behzad Dabu, Morgan McNaught, Terrence Mosley, Margot Bordelon, and Cassy Sanders. We met out of a love for theatre, and your friendship is what I carry with me and will forever.

To the 48th Ward Neighbors for Justice. I found a fresh purpose when I linked up with you, found a home that I didn't know I needed. There are way too many people to thank, so I will briefly say thank you to Mary, Colin, Vino, Dave, Andrew, Nathaniel, Peter, pb, Charlie, Olivia, Margo, Emily, Jamie, Elena, Dom, Taylor, Kristen, Kelly, Jill, Hilesh, Joel, Marilynn, Antonio, and Leah. I really do believe that we will win.

To the wider Chicago activist and organizer community. Thank you for showing all of us what it's like to show up every day and struggle to build something new. The revolution will have joy and abundance, that much is certain.

To the staff and artists of Young Chicago Authors, past and present. I will not pretend that this isn't complicated, but thank you to José Olivarez and Britteney Black Rose Kapri, for believing in me enough to bring me in, and to Mariah, Alyssa, Toaster, Sophie, and Max for making the work feel like home. And to the current staff (Demetrius, Ana, Heather, Matt, Dominique, Luis, E'mon, Jonathan, Mercedes, Laszlo, Sara, Scott, Lynna), no one but us knows what we've been through. I'm proud of our resilience.

In many ways, this book is a critique of everything that has shaped me, and nowhere is this truer than the Chicago restaurant industry. I will never forget both the bullshit and the beauty but mostly the laughter and the shit-talking. A non-exhaustive list of those who have mattered to me includes Jeff, Luis, Antonio, Sam, Alison, Rosie, Brice, Jared, Sal, Tangie, Jessie, and all the people whose names I've changed to protect their identity. And to the owners and entrepreneurs who seek to break the underclass's backs: quit fucking around or this will all get burned to the ground.

To the Dark Noise collective (Nate Marshall, Danez Smith, Aaron Samuels, Franny Choi, Jamila Woods, and of course, Fatimah Asghar). Your work inspired me more than you can ever know, and I miss you more than I ever thought possible.

To Sveta and Yvette. I didn't know that I could have neighbors that could also be friends; thank you for lazy walks and baked goods and being my beacons in the pandemic darkness.

To Aaron Rossini and Patrick Muncie. The only knock against them is that they don't live in Chicago.

To Erika Grammel. You saved my life. I still believe that.

To Matt, Stefanie, Betsy, Will, and Jay. It's amazing and beautiful that we still have each other. There is no place where I'm allowed to be myself more fully than when I'm with you all. Here's to many more decades of friendship. And to Greta, Eleanor, and Paul: I can't wait to see who you become and I hope to be around as long as I can.

To Patti Wheeler and the whole clan: Kathy, Josie, Eddie, and the late Denny Wheeler. Your family has been an extension of my own. To Joshua Hedges, thank you for loving my friend. To

Nicholas Ward

the Myers Family, you will be a part of my life forever.

To my parents. I've never felt like I couldn't pursue the life that I wanted, as rough-and-tumble as it's been. Thank you for that gift.

To Tarah. Thank you for loving me. I do not know what will become of our lives, but I know the journey will be worth it.

Acknowledgments

"Year Zero" was published in *Bird's Thumb*

"The First Game" was published in *Hobart* and their *Baseball Handbook*

A different version of "Sweat" was published in *Vol. 1 Brooklyn*

"There Is No Violence Here" was published in *Catapult*

"Nacional 27" was published in *Hinterland Magazine*

"Johnny's Grill" was published (as "Logan Square: The Best Burger on the Square") in Belt Publishing's *The Chicago Neighborhood Guidebook*

"What Else Do You Do?" was published in *The Billfold*

"Miles Apart" was published (as "Milford, Michigan: So Far Apart") in *Great Lakes Review*

"Paul and Patti and Me" (published as "The Backyard") was originally written and performed for Lifeline Theatre's Fillet of Solo Festival and published in *Post Road*

A different version of "We Travel the City" was written and performed for the Chicago Home Theater Festival

"All Who Belong May Enter" was published in *Midwestern Gothic*

Different versions of "The Match," "The Dresden," "Sweat," "There is No Violence Here," "Steppenwolf," "How to Become (and Stay) Sex Positive," and "Belong Is Where I'm Home" were developed with the Chicago-based 2nd Story storytelling series

New & Forthcoming Releases

American Home by Sean Cho A. · winner of the 2020
Autumn House Chapbook Prize, selected by Danusha Laméris

Under the Broom Tree by Natalie Homer

Molly by Kevin Honold · winner of the 2020 Autumn House
Fiction Prize, selected by Dan Chaon

The Animal Indoors by Carly Inghram · winner of the
2020 CAAPP Book Prize, selected by Terrance Hayes

speculation, n. by Shayla Lawz · winner of the 2020
Autumn House Poetry Prize, selected by Ilya Kaminsky

All Who Belong May Enter by Nicholas Ward · winner of the 2020
Autumn House Nonfiction Prize, selected by Jaquira Díaz

The Gardens of Our Childhoods by John Belk · winner of the 2021
Rising Writer Prize in Poetry, selected by Matthew Dickman

Myth of Pterygium by Diego Gerard Morrison · winner of the
2021 Rising Writer Prize in Fiction, selected by Maryse Meijer

Out of Order by Alexis Sears · winner of the 2021
Donald Justice Poetry Prize, selected by Quincy R. Lehr

Queer Nature: A Poetry Anthology edited by Michael Walsh

For our full catalog, please visit: autumnhouse.org